HURON COUNTY LIBRARY

... FOR A UNIFIED CANADA

*"We must not undervalue our God-given blessings
as a nation to such an extent that we let them
be taken from us as we sleep."*
Major-General (ret'd) Lewis MacKenzie

Canadians have always been perceived as reticent. Or as Maritime writer Lesley Choyce describes us: "a big, shy, slightly embarrassed country." But when faced with the crisis of possible disintegration, fifteen people, from varying backgrounds and from different parts of Canada, have taken the opportunity to speak out on what we have and what we stand to lose.

Each contributor has responded with passion and conviction. Whether from Roberta Bondar's unique perspective in space or Joe Clark writing from South Africa, all are powerful arguments for unity and understanding. There are some wonderful surprises: Laurier LaPierre's time-travel fantasy, Roch Carrier's moving, personal poem. Rounding out the collection are contributions from Matthew Barrett, Neil Bissoondath, Stompin' Tom Connors, Ivan Jaye, Judy Mappin, Matthew Coon Come, Tom Hill, Peter C. Newman and Bob White.

This remarkable collection of heartfelt writing about our nation would be welcome at any time. Coming now, it functions as a wake-up call to every Canadian to have the courage and conviction to speak out and show why we love this country and need to keep it whole.

If You Love This Country

FIFTEEN VOICES FOR A UNIFIED CANADA

Penguin Books

PENGUIN BOOKS
Published by the Penguin Group
Penguin Books Canada Ltd, 10 Alcorn Avenue, Toronto, Ontario, Canada M4V 3B2
Penguin Books Ltd, 27 Wrights Lane, London W8 5TZ, England
Penguin Books USA Inc., 375 Hudson Street, New York, New York 10014, U.S.A.
Penguin Books Australia Ltd, Ringwood, Victoria, Australia
Penguin Books (NZ) Ltd, 182-190 Wairau Road, Auckland 10, New Zealand

Penguin Books Ltd, Registered Offices: Harmondsworth, Middlesex, England

Published in Penguin Books, 1995
1 3 5 7 9 10 8 6 4 2

Copyright © Penguin Books Canada Limited, 1995

Canadian Cataloguing in Publication Data

Main entry under title:

If you love this country: fifteen voices for a unified Canada

Text in English and French with French text on inverted pages.
Title on added t.p.: Pour l'amour de ce pays : quinze voix pour un Canada uni.
ISBN 0-14-025251-7

1. Canada - English-French relations. 2. Canada - Politics and government - 1993-   .*
3. Nationalism - Canada. I. Bissoondath, Neil, 1955-   . I. Title : Pour l'amour de ce pays.

FC98.14 1995   971.064'8   C95-930915-2E

Données de catalogage avant publication (Canada)

Vedette principale au titre:

Pour l'amour de ce pays : quinze voix pour un Canada uni

Texte en francais et en anglais dispose tête-bêche.
Titre de la p. de t. additionnelle : If you love this country: fifteen voices for a unified Canada.
ISBN 0-14-025251-7

1. Canada - Relations entre anglophones et francophones. 2. Canada - Politique et
gouvernement - 1993-   . 3. Nationalism - Canada. I. Bissoondath, Neil, 1955-   .
II. Titre: If you love this country.

FC98.14 1995   971.064'8   C95-930915-2F
F1027.14 1995

The essays by Matthew Barrett, Matthew Coon Come and Bob White have been adapted
from speeches.

Cover photo © Hank de Lespinasse/The Image Bank

Introduction

It is not unsophisticated, as Joe Clark points out, to believe in personal gestures.

As I listened to "As It Happens" one evening in January, I found myself filled with frustration. Politicians and economists were discussing what would happen if Quebec were to choose sovereignty. With cool dispassion, this panel of self-proclaimed experts reviewed the economic, military, and political implications of the breakup of Canada, employing scare tactics with predictable results.

This book is a personal gesture: a collection of passionate voices in the midst of a largely passionless debate. Faced with the upcoming referendum's very real threat to national unity, fifteen Canadians from a variety of backgrounds and regions have rallied to respond. By contributing their perspectives to this special collaborative book, they have boldly, and often with great emotion, spoken about what we have—and what we have to lose. It is evidence that Canadians—citizens of what Maritime writer Lesley Choyce calls "a big, shy, slightly embarrassed country"—care deeply about the survival of our country, and are not nearly as reticent as their own self-image suggests.

If You Love This Country features some of the most beautiful and moving words ever written about Canada—from Roberta Bondar's unique perspective peering down from space, to Joe Clark's eloquent plea composed during a visit to newly united South Africa, to the legendary Stompin' Tom Connors's wise reflections on the land he has travelled and immortalized in song.

There is tough talk from Bob White and Peter C. Newman, poetry from Roch Carrier and a patriotic time-travel fantasy from Laurier LaPierre. And, since this is an issue that touches us all, we've included two pieces by writers heretofore unknown—ordinary Canadians whose words ring every bit as true as those of the book's better-known contributors.

As I write this introduction, it seems for the moment that the separatist momentum is on the wane—that the referendum will be delayed, and that the final vote may well be in favour of unity. But the ongoing success of the Parti Québécois in Quebec tells another story. The truth is, we are looking at a question with a long legacy and, most probably, a troubling future.

Whatever happens in the months ahead, Canadians must look beyond the current crisis and make perfectly clear our active commitment to the integrity and diversity of our country. Let us admire the distinct culture that is Quebec and acknowledge our pride in that culture. Let us reach out—person to passionate person—and affirm our love and respect for this country and its peoples. Let us do what we can for a new, enlightened sense of unity. Let us not be a nation broken nor diminished, but rather a nation reborn.

Cynthia Good
Publisher, Penguin Books Canada Limited
March 1995.

Acknowledgements

This book was made possible by the energy and commitment of many people. First and foremost, I'd like to thank the contributors and those who assist them for responding with such eloquence and speed to the invitation to participate. I'd also like to thank those who would have liked to contribute, but who were forced to reluctantly decline because of schedule constraints. The opportunity to talk with all of you about the future of Canada was inspiring and an experience I will not soon forget.

Special thanks are owed to the terrific team of translators for their dedication, skill and efficiency; to Dianne Craig, who once again faced a preposterous deadline with good humour and dedication; and to project co-ordinator Wendy Thomas, both for her organizational genius and for her commitment to the book.

By chance, Bruce Westwood of Westwood Lord Inc. was the first to hear of the idea for this book—and what a lucky chance that was. He embraced it with enthusiasm and became a kind of partner in its planning, offering practical suggestions, constant encouragement and a willingness to express a love for Canada that fortunately became the norm for everyone involved in this project.

Contents

Spacelog STS42
— Discovery

Roberta L. BONDAR,
O.C., O. Ont., M.D., Ph.D., F.R.C.P.(C)

TRANSMISSION from Earth has extended our stay in orbit for an extra twenty-four hours, circling the planet at a distance of 160 nm. Numerous and not so subtle exchanges have occurred between our crew and ground control over the revised uplinked payload crew activity plan. The extra Earth day and night will not provide us with either much needed rest or with any free time to view the stars or our home planet. It seems harsh treatment for those of us here, aboard *Discovery*, in return for the supreme dedication and long hours in Spacelab that have consumed us. I have survived the training, the launch and life in general, and I need time to savour my dream, for me and for those who can be with me only in spirit.

At times such as these, I wonder if anything will soothe my aching back and cool my tired eyes. In the future, other missions will benefit from our work, but for now, I know that being a pioneer, I am pushing the envelope of space, history and humankind's thinking, not just my Earth-derived body. I have given my everything to this mission, and yet I know that there must be more from me—more discipline, more strength, more energy. I am not able to call on my support systems that are sometimes half a world away. I see only my fellow crew members and hear the business-filled voices from Huntsville and Houston. There is no stirring wake-up music from our comrades on the ground on this flight, as we work around the clock. My hands are those of scientists from countries whose borders I can no longer see.

Our orbits press close to the terminator, where the Earth interposes itself between the invisible rays of sunlight and the vacuum that expands beyond the planet. I know that I will sleep soundly again, albeit briefly, while the Earth and our sun continue their dance as they have throughout human existence and, no doubt, long before and may long after.

Later that day

I am glowing in Earthlight, and filled with its song. The strength is within me, again, flowing through my mind and my muscles.

After the revised schedule appeared on the teleprinter pages, I began to listen to taped music in an attempt to revive my somewhat dampened spirits. But the music, by itself, did not dissolve my focus on the IML-1 payload, nor did it lull me into a time and place far removed from the constant work environment that surrounds me. It was a good idea, but not a great idea. I had played the prerecorded tapes from my support systems earlier in the flight, but now I needed something that was current. I wanted to contact them in real time, to have a conversation, not just to relay work-related words in a one-way stream through NASA Select. At least I had music and a photocopied picture of Ming the Merciless. And without the communication unit's wire clamped around my head, I could have both ears tuned to the same sounds from my cassette tape recorder.

I decided to float up to the flight deck, where my favourite three crew members were hanging about the windows. Only up here does it look normal to see feet, hands, heads and knees all in the same place. I grasped the bottom rung of the ladder in order to pivot upwards from the middeck. A few very familiar bars of music in the head-set of my tape recorder caught my attention as I rotated effortlessly feet-first past all the rungs of the ladder up towards the flight deck. At that moment, "O

Canada" rose from a deep tenor voice on my cassette tape. I was flinging myself towards the top of the mid-deck roof. I managed a corrective roll just in time to tuck my head up into the flight deck before my feet got there, but all the while I was choking away the oppressive lump in my throat. "Our home and native land" was never more beautiful and never more meaningful. As luck and the guiding stars would have it, someone said, "Hey, Bobbie, we're going over Canada." How many Earthlings have ever been afforded the gift of seeing the land of their birth and hearing its united voice? My fatigue slipped into a remote corner of my memory and I could not believe my good fortune. I did not lose presence of mind but explained that I was listening to my national anthem as an excuse for pushing my friends' floating bodies away from the windows for an unobscured view.

Canada is so big, I thought, and yet this planet is so small. The early encounters from space that I had with this land of my birth were literally many moons ago, but they were in snatches, interrupted by calls from the ground, and never for more than two or three minutes at a time. At the speed of eight kilometres a second, the shuttle covers a lot of territory, and the descent or ascent of *Discovery* turns geography into a new course. I recalled a moment earlier in the flight, when an IMAX shot over the Belcher Islands was being set up. The crew couldn't distinguish the swirls of land from the surrounding ice. They asked for my help, and as a bonus, I was able to see northern lakes and rivers that I had touched when I was a medical student, working in Moose Factory. This time we were in a descending orbit across the top of Saskatchewan and Manitoba, arcing our way from north of Lake Winnipeg. There were so few clouds, I noticed, that I was able to focus my eyes southward to a vast tract of darker grey. It occurred to me that Canada *should* be famous for soapstone. The whole country appears to be cut from one giant piece, on these winter days in January.

I rewound the music tape, pressed "play" and at the same time I had my first glimpse of the edge of Lake Superior. There are no borders between lands, as we see it in reality from the distance of space. Provinces and territories are not pink, green, yellow or blue. Sweeping my eyes from what is called Manitoba, Ontario, and into Quebec, I was struck by the similarity of the landscape, and the similarity of my feelings. I could see no one, and when I turned the tape off, there was only silence. But somehow I felt that everyone was looking up. I could sense the many hands that were reaching to heights far above what the confines of Earth allowed them to do. It was as if this massive stone cut with patches of white and shades of grey was living and reaching out to me, cheering me onwards, and it was so familiar, homey and real. This Earthlight from the land below was light from Canada, and it penetrated to the depths of my soul. It overcame the darkness created by the detachment of being removed from Earth. I was reminded that my role on this mission is not just as a scientist or an astronaut. I represent all the things that are possible in Canada—life, education, opportunity, work ethic, values and love. I mustn't tire. Too many people depend on me to show the world our strength, and to show that our spirit will rise.

And there I stayed, clinging to the window frame, trying to memorize each line of white and grey, while I sipped my grapefruit drink. It is interesting, not to see black on the planet by Earth day, when the shuttle is surrounded by black, sprinkled only with the light from countless stars. I saw only shades of grey and white as my eyes swept over the vast terrain of Canada. I couldn't help but smile to myself about living in grey and white, and how Canadians, not unlike other Earthlings, strive to achieve black and white in policies that guide our lives.

The beauty of Canada is rugged yet finely carved by forces greater than most people will ever comprehend. We are positioned on the planet to maximize the effects of seasons, and so we are blessed with variety and challenge. On Earth it is clear that there is sometimes a drive to separate groups historically because most of us don't have the opportunity to see beyond the immediate horizon. It imperils our future. In space, I am philosophical, viewing all the land as a continuous sheet without the social context that human beings impose on the physical surround. It is as if we believe ourselves to be equal to the powerful forces of Earth. In doing so, we allow emotional and cultural values to shape ourselves in isolation, when in reality, the physical forces of Earth ultimately will determine when and where we will survive.

Too quickly, *Discovery* began to leave Canada as it flew over the east coast. The great ice and snow of Newfoundland sharply defined the edge of the last piece of land that I recognized as my home base. The maritime provinces of Nova Scotia, New Brunswick and Prince Edward Island looked to have been cut from this grey and white sheet with a sculptor's tool, giving character to the vast sea to the east. The founders of our country would watch in disbelief to see the Atlantic shrink beneath the nose of this mighty ship. What powerful images there are up here, seeing how close England, France and the rest of Europe are to Canada. The demanding voyages of many months undertaken by early Canadian immigrants can be eclipsed in less than half an hour, here in space.

My Earth-viewing was interrupted by the not-so-stern voice of our commander calling for lights out for those of us on the next shift. It was only five hours until my next eighteen-hour day but I just couldn't leave with the others. I chose to work on the computer to determine how long until the next approach to Canada — from the west, of course. I hadn't seen the west coast, yet, for a variety of reasons: it was night, or I had been tucked away in my sleep restraint, or more likely I had my hands in the glove box in Spacelab. This time I did not want to be denied. I was at the window and knew that if I could hold my position and stay awake for an hour, I would be rewarded by the sight of the snow-capped Rocky Mountains. But even so, in the end, I was thwarted by Earth's weather. Only peaks of snow and rock with an occasional break to reveal a curling white river were all that greeted me from what I assumed was the west coast of Canada. I was convinced, however, that British Columbia lay below and Alberta was not far behind, and now, I had seen more of Canada.

I flip on the tape recorder before I have to return to Spacelab and am settling down with the theme from the *Return of the Jedi.* This is giving me time to reflect on the emotions of the past few minutes. I can grasp the significance of being in space and find myself smiling. In my mind, I touch down to imagine how the west coast and plains indigenous people shape their lives and art through these physical forces. How rich we are to have in our land those who grasp and respect the power of nature. For those of us who were born in Canada to a society created by ideas carried here from other lands, it is too easy to assume a level of sophistication that excludes a different perspective. I have developed new insight into my life on planet Earth. If only everyone could see that there is nothing out here quite like us. Of the wondrous sheets of land on the rotating blue/green planet beyond, the one that protects the people of Canada is the most blessed. There are shorelines, islands, rivers, plains and lots and lots of lakes. True, there is snow, but from the snow we continue to have fresh water that replenishes the large water storage areas of our land.

How odd, that we do not see what we have—it is so clear from here. We in Canada have a common land mass, common history and a common destiny with respect to the physical forces on the planet. These facts alone might bind us together were it not for issues that have developed historically to cope with contemporary society.

From my vantage point far above Earth's blue sky and in the very sunlight that is shared by all Canadians, I know us to be a brave, strong, hard-working nation brought together by history and the physical mass of the land. We share common concerns of fresh air, clean water and good soil. From the west coast through the prairies, central Canada to the east coast, there is no discontinuity. The spaces and changes in elevation that do occur are tiny with respect to the total area we cover in Canada and are minuscule in the global context. And it is all my home.

I am impressed with these feelings, and very impressed that I feel strongly enough to record them. I *enjoyed* being a Canadian before my flight, but now I am *overjoyed* and proud that I share my life with those I left behind in my home and native land. Within one orbit of Earth I have been lifted from fatigue with a rush of energy. I now better understand our native people, their insight and respect for things that other parts of our society speak of conquering. This respect for the environment struggles with the political and economic reality of today's society, as Canada evolves a new identity. By working to combine all our strengths and vision, we can lift our own spirits to become a greater nation, one poised strategically to set examples to the rest of this small planet.

Dr. Roberta L. Bondar, O.C., O.Ont.,
Canadian astronaut, physician and scientist,
flew in space aboard the space shuttle
Discovery *on the First International*
Microgravity Laboratory Mission,
January 22-30, 1992.

A Call to Action

Joe CLARK

I AM writing this in South Africa, where I have been meeting with people who, five years ago, were literally killing one another. Today, they are sitting down together to draft a constitution that will let them build a common future. It is too early to know if they will succeed or fail.

But, already, they have held the first election in their history where every citizen could vote; formed a coalition government of national unity, led by a black president, with his white predecessor serving as a deputy president; and agreed on a remarkable interim constitution.

Of course, Canada and South Africa are profoundly different communities.

But, on the surface, South Africans face some challenges familiar to Canadians. There are communities that would prefer to separate, rather than share a country. There is a strong minority that fears its distinctive culture may be overwhelmed. There is a debate about how much power should rest with the central government, and how much with the parts. There is a rich resource base, and a sense of great potential waiting to be realized, but serious economic disparities exist among the regions. There are different languages, cultures, expectations.

However, on at least two counts, our countries are markedly different.

First, their divisions are deep, and real, and reinforced by the bloody recent memory of killing, fear and hatred. By contrast, our differences in Canada are eminently manageable.

And second, they are sitting down co-operatively to seek a new way to live together, while we Canadians appear to be drifting further apart.

The great irony in Canada is that our national community is at serious risk, and yet we have no real divisions.

I have been privileged to serve more than twenty years in Canadian public life, including an intensive period when I was directly responsible for constitutional negotiations. I have been into every part of every province and territory, and talked and listened to thousands of Canadians.

Throughout that experience, I have not seen a single issue of substance that was insurmountable. There are no fundamental divisions in Canada. There is no irreconcilable difference, no "show-stopper."

There are, of course, different views—about the appropriate power of the central government, or the appropriate role of the province of Quebec as the safeguard of the Quebec community, or the rights of the aboriginals, or the Senate, or a thousand other important details.

In my judgment, many of these issues are urgent and cannot simply be shunted aside. The status quo doesn't work—not for Quebec, nor for aboriginals, nor many western Canadians—so it is idle to pretend these pressures will go away, or that they have been "stirred up by politicians" and so are artificial.

They are real issues, but they are not irreconcilable differences, neither singly nor together. None is so fundamental that it should cause a country to fail—particularly not a country that, by any objective standard, serves its citizens so well. Nor does the sum of those differences warrant breaking up the country that the United Nations regularly judges "the best place in the world to live," and embarking on the gamble of trying to build something new in the bitter wake of failure.

Yet, since 1980, the tensions within Canada have grown more serious, more numerous, more threatening. Our attempts to reconcile our manageable differences have not only failed but, by failing, have exaggerated our sense of separateness and conflict.

Why is that? I think there are two basic factors.

The first is that at least one of the significant parties has always wanted the discussion settled on its terms, and so was not interested in a real accommodation. In the early 1980s, the Trudeau government would not contemplate a solution that involved a substantial increase in the power of Quebec or other provinces. And, today, the Parizeau government will not contemplate a solution short of "sovereignty."

The second reason is that the discussion has been in terms that meant different things to different people. Phrases like "special status" or "distinct society" became angry symbols of division, but often were not analyzed or judged on their merit. Those disputes happened often enough that they deepened a sense of division between Canadians in Quebec and Canadians in the rest of the country. We regularly interpreted the same event in opposite ways.

For example, the 1982 constitutional reform was embraced outside Quebec because it promised a charter of rights designed to appeal to Canadians who believed their equal treatment needed to be guaranteed formally, and a patriation proposal that was seen as the final cutting of colonial ties with England. But these were not the issues in Quebec, where the proposal was overwhelmingly rejected because it did nothing significant about the powers of provinces or the identity of Quebec (and, moreover, it was achieved in a notorious "deal" that cut out the premier of Quebec).

The Meech Lake Accord was seen in Quebec as a simple, and minimal, guarantee of the status of Quebec within Canada—an act of inclusion. Outside Quebec, the Meech Lake Accord became seen as a symbol of exclusion—secret meetings among "men in suits"; no progress on aboriginals, women, the north, the Senate; a "deal" among "insiders."

The "Distinct Society" was seen in Quebec as a simple affirmation of reality, and outside Quebec as special status.

Those conflicting images are important, because the present division in this country is not about competing views of federalism. It is about words and symbols—"rejection," "special status," "Meech Lake."

What will be decisive is the assessment of ordinary Canadians as to the question: "Is Canada so fundamentally divided that we cannot live and grow together?" By any objective standard, that is an absurd proposition. There are fundamentally divided societies in this world, where people kill one another or react to their neighbours with hatred or fear. There is virtually none of that here—no historic hatreds, none of the fears and antagonisms that pull communities apart.

Our experience, in fact, has been the opposite. As a practical matter, most Canadians have not had much actual contact with one another. Our impressions of our fellow citizens are second-hand. Very few Quebeckers have much direct experience with life in western Canada, or even in Ontario or the Atlantic provinces. And vice versa. What we know is what we hear, and often that is inflammatory or wrong. In the absence of actual experience, many Canadians form their impressions of their fellow citizens on the basis of newscasts reporting spectacular excesses, like wiping feet on a flag or urging easterners to freeze in the dark, or angry perceptions of the "Distinct Society" or the "rejection" of Meech Lake.

The perceptions might be wrong, but the anger is real. The best way to lance the anger is to correct the impression. And the best way to do that is for individual Canadians to become actively involved, right now, in the debate about the nature and the future of our country.

Joe CLARK   *15*

Canada's basic problem is that our citizens do not understand one another's point of view. To paraphrase Will Rogers, our problem is not what we don't know; our problem is that the things we know are wrong. The only real solution is for individual citizens to check their own prejudices and challenge the prejudices of others.

It has probably been a mistake to call these discussions about Canada "constitutional discussions." The very word "constitution" freezes people, turns them off. Constitutions are for lawyers and for governments; they are the forms we give to agreements about what kind of country we are.

So this debate is not about a constitution. It is about a country—a country that belongs to all of us, and whose future will be decided by what we do—or what we fail to do.

At the moment, one province will have a referendum in which they will cast a judgment as to whether they want to stay in Canada. If we want to be legalistic and irrelevant, we might argue that their decision is not binding upon the rest of us, that no one province has the power to break up the country. That argument is worse than a waste of time because it only angers the people who are going to vote and makes them more likely to feel unwelcome in Canada.

The reality is that if a large Canadian province, after a long debate, votes to leave Canada, that decision would throw everything into question. Lawyers could argue until their bank accounts bulged, but the fact would be that the country would be on the road either to break-up or to dramatic change.

So the immediate question is not whether Quebec has the right to leave, but rather: Why would Quebec want to leave?

And although that is a question only Quebeckers will

answer, it is one that all of us can influence.

We—you and I and our children and our friends—are the Canada Quebeckers are being asked to leave. What do those Quebeckers know about you, or your family, or your community? What have you told them?

Or are you leaving it to Preston Manning and Jacques Parizeau, Jean Chrétien and Lucien Bouchard to speak for you?

I believe that the principal source of separatism in Quebec is the sense, among the ordinary people of that province, that they are not really wanted in the rest of Canada. They take personally the "rejection" of the Meech Lake Accord, the criticism of the "Distinct Society." And in many cases, that negative news is all they know of Canada. They have no personal connections, no frame of reference within which they might judge those harsh impressions.

They are prepared to believe bad news about Canada because they haven't heard much good news. In fact, now that there is a separatist government in Quebec, when something good is said about Canada, Parizeau explains it away.

So why don't you give Quebeckers some good news? Why don't you tell them about your family, your community, the landscape you know, the country you love?

Why not—in this season when Quebeckers are deciding whether to leave our country—reach out to people in Quebec, as you might reach out to a new neighbour who has moved in down the street?

Some of my critics say I am unsophisticated to believe that personal gestures like that might make some difference. I know they make a difference. I have seen it happen, time after time after time.

The problem is to encourage more people to make these gestures.

The easiest thing to do is visit Quebec. We don't know when the referendum will be called. It may be delayed until the fall, which creates a summer of opportunities for Canadians who are going to take their holidays somewhere, to go into Quebec, to ask about the language and the culture, to talk about Canada.

And if the referendum comes earlier, or you can't arrange to travel, find other ways to reach out to the Canadians who will vote on our country's future. Get in touch with the Council for Canadian Unity. Organize friends to take out ads or join letter-writing campaigns or simply start the practice of speaking well of our extraordinary country.

It is no exaggeration to speak of Canada in those terms. We are an extraordinary country. When Canadians are required to deal with different languages, different cultures, different expectations—we do that very successfully. The mutual respect we boast about actually exists, in most circumstances where different Canadians come together. That is the fact, but not the perception.

In a sense, we are ill-served by our good fortune. Canada is a rich and lucky society, taking our advantages for granted, assuming we can survive any shock, deriding the qualities of compromise and accommodation that the world sees as our trademark. The result is that our population has a limited personal experience of either how easy it is to work together or how necessary, and an exaggerated sense of what divides us.

That is a dangerous combination, likely to become more volatile. Within Quebec, Mr. Parizeau and his associates will certainly build on the sense that Quebec is unwelcome and constrained in the Canadian family, and that everyone would be happier apart.

The atmosphere outside Quebec has been remarkably calm, even placid. *Indépendantistes* trolling for dramatic over-reaction have had little success. So far. As the rhetoric rises in Quebec, there will be a powerful temptation for political leaders, or business people, or "analysts," or citizens responding to ubiquitous polls, to take hard lines. This would not only harm the federalist cause in a referendum but could lock in attitudes that could limit the accommodations that will have to come after a referendum, particularly if independence is rejected.

More serious than a hard-line statement today is the cavalier attitude many Canadians take towards the consequences of splitting the country. They equate it to a run on the dollar or a hurricane or flood—unpleasant, but temporary.

That assumes that Canadian pragmatists would arrange a hasty, happy divorce; that the boundaries of a departing Quebec would not be contested; and that international markets would give Canada time to work out our little problem.

Everything I know tells me that any negotiation about share of the debt or boundaries would be long, bitter and debilitating. And no one can predict the reaction of the money markets. Mexico proved the perils of an international economy in which one shock can trigger a crisis, and it would be well for cavalier Canadians to consider what the shock of a vote to split Canada would do to investment plans in Alberta or Ontario, or the credit ratings of Saskatchewan or Manitoba, or Atlantic Canada.

The stakes are higher now than they were in 1980.

Fifteen years ago, there was a benign attitude in the rest of Canada about events in Quebec and a benign attitude in the world about Canadian unity. We cannot assume either today.

It is commonplace to observe that a much harder line has developed in the rest of the country. Sadly, knowledge of Quebec and its case has not increased, but frustration and impatience have. In part, that is a direct result of the insistence of Quebec leaders on looking inwards and the failure of various national governments and "conventional wisdom" to place the Quebec question in the context of a larger Canadian dissatisfaction with the constitutional status quo.

The "status quo" is an interesting notion in Canada. In fact, in this era of transforming changes, there is never a status quo. There is always change, but it is often incremental, at the margins. That is acceptable to Canadians who profit from or are generally comfortable with arrangements as they are.

Over the last thirty years, large identifiable Canadian communities have come to believe that their interests suffer from "arrangements as they are," and they will not accept merely incremental change. That is certainly the case among the large number of western Canadians who believe that traditional institutional arrangements in Canada leave them out. It is indisputably the case with aboriginal Canadians, who believe both that they are abused by the present system, and that their basic rights are not recognized. And in Quebec—among separatists, nationalists and most federalists—there is a conviction that their security as a community depends on the province where francophones are a majority having more authority over their destiny.

In an atmosphere characterized by rising tensions but no real debate, it would not be surprising if more Quebeckers come to believe they are not much wanted in Canada, and if citizens in Alberta, or British Columbia, or Ontario come to believe that Quebec could never be satisfied in Canada. Those impressions would be strongest among Canadians who had little real contact with one another. But that is the common experience in this long-distance country. Lucien Bouchard has never been more representative of Canadians than when he admitted that he did not know "the rest" of his country very well. Most premiers, most business leaders, many commentators, most legislators throughout Canada could say the same thing. The question is whether we can reach over the perceptions of division to see whether we really disagree.

My experience leads me to believe that there is a great deal of agreement in Canada about the kind of new federation we need.

To some degree, that potential consensus on substance has existed for some time and has been obscured by the disputes about terms and by a powerful conventional wisdom, outside Quebec, that any reduction in the power of the central government would imperil "the Canadian idea." But that potential consensus is also being influenced by two new realities — fiscal pressures, which make it impossible to sustain the degree of duplication and *dirigisme* that had become the norm in Canada; and the new insistence on having more decisions made more locally.

That affects directly the debate about where powers should lie in the modern Canadian federation—and that is the crucial debate for Quebec. My strong view is that, if we could get beyond the war of words and caricatures, we would find a large agreement in the country—among leaders and among citizens—that significantly more power should be vested in provincial governments.

That would require important conditions—for example, if Ottawa were to step back from significant programs and services it provides now, there would need to be a willingness in the wealthier provinces to have Canada maintain acceptable standards in the less wealthy. There would almost certainly need to be some special arrangements—equivalent to the "special status" we now accord education in Newfoundland, and language rights in New Brunswick, or the Quebec Pension Plan, or the guarantee of parliamentary seats for smaller provinces and territories—and take account of special circumstances that exist in some provinces and not in others. Most fundamentally, the central government would need the power to function effectively in a competitive and changing modern world. Of course, there would be intense debate about all these issues, but if we could have that debate on its merits, I am convinced there would be broad nation-wide support for a significantly less centralized federation.

It is legitimate for sovereignists to respond: "If that's so, why hasn't it happened so far?" There are two answers.

First, it has happened. By definition, a federal system is flexible. Unquestionably, many Quebeckers believe the status quo is too confining for the society that modern Quebec has become, but it is also beyond dispute that federalism has given Quebec a lot of room—the Quebec Pension Plan, its own system of student loans, its own schools, its own design of family allowances; the power to collect its own taxes, select its own immigrants, build up *les Caisses de Dépôt*, establish Hydro-Québec, Radio-Québec and its own representatives in foreign capitals. What is much more significant than those past accomplishments is the fact that, for the last fifteen years, in constitutional discussions, governments, political parties and commentators outside Quebec have, for their own reasons, moved even closer to Quebec's vision of a less centralized Canada. Provinces like Alberta and British Columbia—which are sometimes portrayed as "anti-Quebec"—have regularly made constitutional proposals that would increase the relative power of the province. The Charlottetown Accord reflected a much broader willingness to move in that direction. Premier Harcourt of British Columbia has renewed some of those proposals in recent months.

The second answer to skeptical sovereignists is precisely the broad change in public attitude created by fiscal realities and the desire for local control.

Parizeau limited his process to *"consultations sur l'avenir du Quebec."* But that question cannot be addressed honestly without an assessment of the attitudes of the rest of Canada. Three critical issues were left out of Parizeau's exercise.

First, the tension between Quebec and other Canadians is not based on disagreements about substance and, in fact, obscures a broad range of common views and values.

Second, federalism is flexible enough to give Quebec more real room now, and there is a clear and accelerating consensus in other provinces for a decentralization of powers.

Third, fiscal realities force governments to redefine federalism, and the growing desire for community control makes that tendency irresistible.

Would the Chrétien government move in that direction? Fiscal realities face it too, whatever its constitutional preferences. Moreover, the long shadow of the Trudeau era may have less influence now on self-described pragmatists forming a majority government of their own and trying to cope with a nation in transformation.

And, in any event, modern governments take account of public opinion, and public attitudes towards centralized authority have changed.

It is important, in the next few months, that our focus should not be simply on winning a referendum, because the question could be ambiguous or the result close, and that would mean a debate would begin again about whether Quebec would leave or stay. Indeed, the focus should not just be on Quebec.

As I reflect on our failures to achieve constitutional reform, I become more convinced that a central mistake has been to cast this as a debate about Quebec. It is about Canada—a changed Canada in which Quebec will feel at ease and at home, and so will other Canadians whose legitimate interests are not well-served now.

Obviously, helping Quebeckers feel at home in their large country will be a major part of the challenge— maybe *the* major part.

But what must change is the attitude that the "Quebec question" is the only "real question," and that the other issues are more or less incidental. Whatever their denials, that has been the attitude of official Ottawa and most of the so-called "national" commentators, for as long as I can remember.

Of the four Canadians since 1968 who became prime minister by winning a national election, I am the only one who did not come from Quebec. I am sympathetic to the province—some would say too sympathetic—but my formative view of Canada occurred elsewhere.

I met Stoney Indians before I met a Quebecker and imbibed the sense of alienation of the prairies before I ever heard of the "Quiet Revolution." The great majority of Canadians in the communities where I grew up spoke English and, if they didn't, more spoke German or Chinese than French. So, inevitably, I saw Canada through Alberta eyes, Quebec through Canadian eyes. It is not at all surprising that prime ministers, and their advisers, who grew up in the heart of Hugh MacLennan's "Two Solitudes" would see Canada through Quebec eyes.

It has been natural to see the "Quebec issue" as the principal question facing Canada. No other province contemplates separation. Nowhere else was a Pierre

Laporte kidnapped and killed. Nowhere else are the differences so clear.

But the reality about Canada is that we have changed profoundly in several of our communities. There is nothing inherently threatening about that. It is inevitable in the modern world.

What strikes one in South Africa is the consensus that seems to unite parties who were so recently at one another's throats. What strikes one in Canada is the basic consensus that has always been here, but rarely mobilized. Ours is the easier challenge, if we have the will to respond to it.

And that is up to you.

❦

*Joe Clark was a member of the
House of Commons for twenty-one years,
serving as prime minister, secretary of state
for external affairs and minister responsible
for constitutional affairs.*

Two Characters
in Search
of an Author

❧

Laurier L. LaPierre,
O.C.

WE are in the year 1756! Spugliguel, the guardian angel of spring, has allowed Ambriel, one of the princes of the Order of Thrones, to unwind the month of May.

I am standing on the north-east shore of the St. Lawrence River where it meets another river called Saguenay in the country of Canada to whose people I belong. As I'm watching the whales frolicking around and wondering how on earth I'm going to get across to Tadoussac, situated some seventy leagues below the town of Quebec, a Native in a canoe appears out of nowhere and says to me in French, "My name is Mascou. Come with me!" And so I do.

Mascou is about twenty-five years old, six foot five inches tall, weighing about 175 pounds. He is of a rich and expensive copper colour. His black hair is long and tied in a pony-tail, his nose is finer and his lips thinner than what I am accustomed to see on aboriginals, and his eyes are as deep a black as the deepest pool in the ocean. He wears a leather vest, which hardly hides his healthy torso, tight leather pants, moccasins, but, thank the gods, no feathers.

He teaches me to paddle and together we cross the wide expanse of the Saguenay and come to rest at Tadoussac. That's where he tells me he belongs to no tribe, no nation, but to all of them.

Like me, he is a lone traveller through time!

Indeed, if truth be told, a Mascou has always been on the go throughout the history of humans on the plot of land we call America. "When the ice covered the land," the memory banks belonging to the Mascou I have just met recount, "Mascou's people came down the corridor between the two ice sheets that blanketed most of the continent we are now in. They were following the great beasts that were their sustenance. It took them about one thousand of your years to effect the journey to the great plains in the south. Along the way some stopped their descent southward and moved, instead, east and west, forming clans and tribes and nations with languages of their own, different ways of doing things and distinct religious rituals. Those who continued further south also founded civilizations and, eventually, they reached the southernmost tip of the continent. It was a long, long journey."

"What happened to all the Mascous?" I ask the Memory.

"The first ones went as far south as the land would permit and the others who followed made their way back north, travelling east and west along the way."

"Why didn't they settle like the others?"

"The Mascous are wanderers and travellers. They stop for only a short time to rest, to procreate and to establish roots. Then they move on, leaving their families behind. The eldest son is always called Mascou and inherits the mission."

"The quest, you mean," I say more to myself than to the Memory. Mascou is by then asleep and dreaming.

In his dreams, he tells me what he (and therefore the collective Mascou) has been up to for the past millennia. He has been everywhere. He has carved totems with the Haidas in their kingdom in the Pacific, erected an inuk-shuk, a pile of stones arranged "in the form of a man" to tell whoever will hear that he and his Inuit companions had been there, celebrated potlaches with the Tsimshian kings on the Skeena River, and by the shores of the most beautiful sound in the world he made love with a Squamish maiden and rested a while. Later, as the ice receded, he travelled from west to east hunting and fishing, tobogganing, snowshoeing and canoeing. He built a life trading with some fine partners and avoided rivalry and war.

Together, Mascou and I relive the arrival of Christopher Columbus to this continent. We both don't enjoy the experience. But the pain continues for there was a Mascou present when a four-legged Hernando Cortés destroyed Montezuma's Aztec empire in 1520 in an orgy of destruction unparalleled in the history of the continent.

In his dreams, Mascou remembers the Vikings at L'Anse aux Meadows in Newfoundland where Freydis Eriksdottir, the bastard daughter of Leif Erikson, axed to death some of the women who had come with her from Greenland. Over half a millennium later, a Mascou was on the banks of the Gaspé peninsula and watched the Mohawk chief Donnacona take Jacques Cartier, the French explorer, to his own Kanata Kon. Mascou was also at the founding of Port Royal in 1605 and became a member of Samuel de Champlain's Order of Good Cheer. He cannot remember but he may have had a part in Marc Lescarbot's *Théâtre de Neptune* in 1606. By May 14, 1607, he had travelled south, to a marshy peninsula in Virginia this time, to attend the London Company's take-over of the continent in the name of James I.

Then he came north again to join Samuel de Champlain in building his *habitation* at the "point of Quebec." Wherever Champlain went, he followed and frequently warned the "founder" of Canada of the consequences should the Iroquois become the enemies of the French. Champlain didn't listen and there followed a century of terrible warfare. While it lasted, Mascou, in 1682, descended the Mississippi to its mouth where Robert Cavelier, Sieur De La Salle, named all the lands he could see Louisiana. Mascou rested there for a while and had a family. In that way he was able to be a member of the party that greeted the *Canadien* Jean-Baptiste le Moyne, Sieur de Bienville, at the founding of New Orleans in 1718.

A few years later, in 1731, a Mascou, travelling through the western lands of the Crees and the Assiniboines, met the famous *Canadien* explorer, Pierre Gaultier de Varennes et de La Vérendrye. By the early 1750s, Mascou, by then an old man, returned to Quebec from the west, bringing with him a son, my Mascou. Both came to the north shore of the St. Lawrence, a few miles down from Quebec. There the father died and "the mission is now mine," Mascou tells me as we approach the shore of St. Joachim.

"When do you take it up?"

"Oh! later. There'll be plenty of time. Canada is here to stay." He looks around and says as we disembark, "My mistress is over there speaking with that little man in the blue uniform." And he's gone!

I've seen her often. Her name is Eloise de Melançon, born in the town of Quebec in 1709, the eldest daughter of Pierre Pommereau de Pidou and Jeanne-Catherine de Chavigny. On June 24, 1725, she married Charles de Melançon, a *Canadien*, an officer in the *Troupes Franches de la Marine* and the seigneur of a large seigneurie, *La Terre du Nord*, which occupies most of the north shore of the St. Lawrence. He is four years older than she is.

Ever since the arrival of the first seigneur in 1636, a Melançon has always lived on the seigneurie to tame the forest, clear the land, till the soil, nurture the community that numbers 2,338 souls (including two hundred "Indians"), suffer the French and placate the God all the colonists worship. A recent census of the seigneurie lists 250 households, 36,750 *arpents* under cultivation, 225 horses, 375 oxen, 290 cows, 697 calves and 1,000 sheep.

By the time of this story, only three of the seven children she bore have survived: an estranged son, Philippe, who lives in Boston and has not been in contact with the family for over a decade; Elisabeth, a vivacious and beautiful twenty-two-year-old young woman; and Charles, who is eighteen and wants to be a priest.

A born traveller, Eloise is much like Mascou, visiting France often and the English colonies to the south. She and her husband correspond with the best minds in Europe and America, and the library at their manor house is even superior to the Jesuits'.

As I approach her, she is still talking with and being charming to the portly little man in blue. I find her very intriguing. She is tall and handsome, with dark brown eyes that camouflage well the passion she is capable of. She exudes authority to the peril of those who dismiss her as an insignificant housewife. I am told that she has a keen sense of revenge, which she couples with a rare generosity of spirit. Her hair is always piled high on her head and she always dresses with taste. And she worries constantly about the fate of the Canada she loves so much.

When I get to her, she is helping the little man into a two-wheeled *calèche* and sends him on his way, preceded by a runner who will clear the road for him and also tell the *curé* of Château Richer that he is to have a guest for dinner.

Turning to me she bows a greeting. I nod my admiration.

"He is, you will be pleased to know, Louis-Joseph Marquis de Montcalm, seigneur de Saint-Véran, Candiac, Tournemire, Vestric, Saint-Julien and Arpajon; Baron de Gabriac, and lieutenant-general. His Most Christian Majesty, Louis XV, in his kindness has sent him to deliver us from the English and their American colonists, who are snipping at our heels." She looks at me and adds, "He wanted to commandeer a *calèche* to take him to Quebec—he is most anxious to start on his mission. I loaned him mine." She smiles charmingly and then with heavy sarcasm she goes on, "The French are very annoying. They speak to us, *Canadiens*, as if we were their peasants in France!"

Walking up the hill back to her chores, she asks more in a statement than in a question, "You have come from far away?"

"Close to 250 years."

She stops and turns, facing me, and says, "So you know what happens to us."

I have the feeling that she too knows.

"Please do not tell me. Let *me* tell you!"

She sits on a wagon and drinks, along with me, some water someone has brought us.

"We have lived here on this land of Canada almost one hundred and fifty years now. During all that time, we have known only forty-two years of peace. This war that has just begun and brought the Marquis here so far from his beloved Provence is the third one this century. My children have lived all their lives waiting for one war to end and another to start." She shifts and puts down her cup before adding, "But we survived them all and will do so again and again. My husband, whom you will probably meet..." She stops and looks intently at me. In my eyes she sees that I shall never meet Charles de Melançon. An immense sadness fills her. But she recovers quickly and continues, "We have survived the Iroquois. The English have always been sent empty-handed before, and we have kept the American colonists in their narrow strip of land by the Atlantic, thus denying them the west. My husband, who has been practically to this other ocean past three ranges of mountains, tells me that it is a land of plenty and of incredible beauty. I believe that, and one day our ownership of it all will be confirmed."

She breathes deeply and appears disoriented. She closes her eyes and before opening them again, she says, "The French may lose the war that is barely beginning, I do not know. But it does not matter! In time, as well, others will threaten us and some of our own people will betray us. That too we shall overcome."

She rises from what has become her throne. Taking in all that lies around her, she whispers softly, "This, the land of Canada, shall always be our inheritance and that of our children!"

She gives me her hand. I kiss it reverently. She begins to walk away, but, no doubt sensing that something is troubling me, she returns to pat my arm. "Canada shall endure! Be well!"

She pats me again and resumes her journey towards Mascou who is waiting for her by the waters of the St. Lawrence.

In due course, Mascou travels west to encounter the railroad, confront Louis Riel, march with Gabriel Dumont and sire another Mascou.

In due course, Eloise de Melançon dies on the Plains of Abraham protecting the French army from the English during the French's ignominious rout from the field of battle.

In due course, I return to the second half of the last decade of the twentieth century certain that *my Canada shall be!*

❧

*Laurier LaPierre tries to be a writer
who likes living in Canada.*

The Liberation of Quebec?

Stompin'
Tom CONNORS

WHAT? Not another Quebec separation referendum? I thought the question was settled fifteen years ago in the last referendum.

It seems to me that Mr. Parizeau and his separatist friends are planning to play Russian roulette with the people of Quebec for as many times as it takes to spin the chamber of his pistol until that one bullet of destruction is finally fired. If he doesn't win the referendum this time, he'll just hold another one, and another one. The law of averages says he's bound to succeed some time.

I'm sure he's heard of the statement attributed to Abraham Lincoln: "You can fool all the people some of the time, and some of the people all the time, but you cannot fool all the people all of the time." I guess, since his recent election, he figures he'd better hold another referendum now, while he's still in a position to "fool all the people some of the time." Maybe this time the bullet of destruction will finally destroy the one and only democratic country in the world that would even allow such a referendum to be held in the first place.

If he's successful, he and his cronies will of course be able to set up their own kind of democracy in a sovereign Quebec. And you can bet your boots that nobody else in this new country of Quebec will ever again be allowed to even mention the word "separate," never mind hold a referendum that plans to make it a reality.

Parizeau has said he doesn't want to change the Canadian system, he wants to get out of it. Well, why doesn't he just do that? Why don't he and the rest of his separatist pals move to some other country like the former Yugoslavia, for instance, where everybody believes in separatism?

I believe the Quebec separatists are much smarter

than that. They want to turn the best democratic system in the world against itself by promising the voters of Quebec that they will be much better leaving Canada and forming their own federal government. And what kind of government would that be, I wonder? And who would it be run by? It would be run by all the Great Quebec Liberators, of course—all the new self-proclaimed heroes who led the poor, down-trodden people of Quebec to freedom from the oppressive Canadian system. It would be run by those who would take off their separatist masks and show themselves for what they really are—sovereignists, complete with their crowns of regal authority.

In my view, it is the ultimate goal of the separatists to become an elite aristocracy in their own little country of Quebec where, far away from the interference of Ottawa and the rest of Canada, they'll be answerable to no one but themselves.

And why is this my view? Because the only people who stand to gain from Quebec separation are the separatists themselves and, perhaps to a much lesser extent, the people who jump out of the frying pan into the fire to support them. The great majority of the people would live to regret it. Once gone from Canada, they'd never get back. By the time they woke up and realized the damage they had done to themselves, the very democratic mechanism that enabled them to separate in the first place would have long since been abolished. And even though the rest of Canadians at that time would no doubt be sympathetic towards their predicament, there would be absolutely nothing we could do to help. By then, the ruling aristocratic oligarchy, i.e., the former separatists, would have made sure of that. And of course, their own armed forces would be standing by to crush anybody foolhardy enough to revolt or rebel.

If you think this is far-fetched, then consider the following. In a true democracy, all the power is vested in the people. They have the right to a free press, which is obligated to keep them thoroughly informed about their options and must not in any way be manipulated by their government representatives. This enables each person to cast a vote for or against any proposal based on his knowledgeable opinion as to what option is best for him. Any person who is not adequately informed can often be convinced to cast a vote against his own best interests. Any party that seeks to gain power or pass legislation with the aid of an uninformed or misguided electorate has absolutely no respect for the democratic process. And those who don't respect it can hardly be expected to perpetuate it.

Recent experiences with free trade, GST, Meech Lake and Charlottetown still remind us of what can happen to a person or a party that, by the way of inadequate information, tries to sell the people a bill of goods. Where are they today? Wherever they are, I'm sure they know that democracy is still alive and well in Canada.

Our democracy works, and we must always be on guard to keep it that way. And because all our other rights are dependent on our right to vote, we must always make sure we are given the proper and factual information that will enable us to vote intelligently. Whenever we vote without knowing the facts, not only do we take the chance of losing some of our rights, we also take the chance of losing our democracy.

Now, who in their right mind would want to do that? It is my contention that the people of Quebec may lose it unwittingly. Why? Because a very large segment of the Quebec population, for various reasons, is totally uninformed about the rest of this great nation to which they presently belong, and the true sentiments of its multicultural population rarely get expressed by media who are

If You Love This Country

themselves afraid to be castigated by the separatists.

Just one example of this: I have recently been informed that twelve out of fourteen Quebec radio stations who were contacted by my record company and asked to play my recent release of a song called "Suzanne De Lafayette" refused on the grounds that "Stompin' Tom is known to be too much of a nationalist, and the playing of his song over the air might disturb too many separatists who would call the stations to complain." This was the reaction, even in light of the fact that the song promotes and encourages the French fact in North America, is sung in both French and English and is co-written by a French person born in Quebec who actually taught me how to sing and correctly pronounce all the words in the French segments. Is this paranoia or what? And what are they afraid of?

They're afraid of the facts, that's what. They preach to their people that separatism is the only way their French language and culture can ever be safeguarded and protected against the rest of Canada whose only inclination, according to them, is to eventually erode and destroy it. They preach that the only way the Quebec people can ever be free to pursue their own best interests is to form their own country and leave their destiny in the hands of the separatists. "You can't trust the Canadian democracy," they advocate, "but you can trust us." (Even though they're not giving you the straight goods, even-handedly.)

Maybe it's time for the people of Quebec to hear some straight facts on the matter. In the first place, French is an official language in this country and must be respected and honoured everywhere you go. And for anyone to be afraid that too many English words may infiltrate the French language and thereby render it less pure, history has shown that the very opposite is the case. I have recently read a book by Charles Berlitz, who is an expert on languages, and was surprised to learn that something less than 10 percent of the English language is actually made up of Anglo-Saxon words. The rest is made up of words from other languages. And wouldn't you just know it: a full 45 percent of what we have come to think of as English just so happens to be French or French derivatives. That is one huge amount of infiltration of just one language into another. But I don't hear any English-speaking persons crying foul.

Of course, the separatists may have another motive for wanting to exclude English from Quebec. And it's not so much for the purpose of protecting the purity of the French language as it is to screen and prevent as much information as possible coming in from the rest of Canada. Oh, you can bet your life that if some radical stomps on a Quebec flag, the information will get through immediately. But if a thousand people express their appreciation and respect for the vibrant French culture, which they sincerely hope will always thrive not only in Quebec but throughout Canada, the chances of the information getting through to the right people are next to nil.

Under the guise of protecting French language and culture, the separatists are using them to isolate a large segment of the Canadian population for the purpose of taking these people away from the very land that is their birthright, a land that they now possess and may pass on to their children for many generations to come, a land in which they have the privilege to come and go, live and love, work and play wherever and whenever they want, without ever having to be looked upon as a stranger. This is not only a land they own, but a great frontier of opportunity that was painstakingly opened up by the sheer fortitude of their courageous forefathers whose names are still proudly emblazoned on our rivers, lakes and streams, and on countless towns and landmarks throughout the nation, no matter where you go. I can't imagine what those men would say today about those who would dare to advocate that this fair and bountiful land should now be abandoned by those to whom it was bequeathed. I believe they would consider it pure cowardice to even suggest such a notion.

If this land was worth the blood and the death of even one French-Canadian soldier, it's at least got to be worth all the courage we can muster up to defeat this cancer called separatism. Quebec must not just pick up and run away from this land simply because it doesn't always get everything it wants from Ottawa. Other provinces don't always get what they want, either, but that is the nature of any democracy. I'll bet my bottom dollar that if Quebec separates from Canada, it will wind up with one hell of a lot less than it has now. And so will the rest of us.

We'll not only lose economically, but disputes of all kinds will flare up everywhere. First Nations, farmers, mining and lumber companies will fight over land borders. Fishermen will fight over the best fishing grounds. Airline companies will fight over air space. Trucking companies and tourists will fight over a corridor of free passage from Ontario to the Maritimes. The scenarios are endless.

What happens if someone gets killed during one of these disputes? Will it lead to resentment and hatred? Will it lead first to border clashes and then to war? Will we have Canadians and former Canadians killing one another? And will we have our war dead who fought for the peace, safety and sanity of this country, as well as for the world, turning in their graves to see the chaos and carnage we got ourselves into by listening to a few separatist hot heads?

No one likes to hear this kind of talk. But remember, it takes only the careless use of a harmless match to burn

---

a house down. And as Canada is house and home to all of us, if we're not careful we could find ourselves walking around in the cold, just lucky enough to still have our lives, should it all go up in smoke.

The Parizeau Experiment, as far as I'm concerned, is no different than a curious, delinquent child, running around with a match, looking for someplace to strike it. And as well-meaning and innocent-looking as he appears to be, he is in fact a menace to the whole family.

In the summer of 1992, I took my son and my wife (who was born in Quebec, incidentally) on a trip to Europe. We also took along another couple (the Quebec-born co-writer of the song I mentioned previously, and his wife, who is also French). While we were there, we drove through many countries, including France, where we spent a good deal of our time. One afternoon we went to Dieppe to visit the Canadian War-Dead Memorial and Cemetery. To any of you who have never been there, I strongly suggest that you pay it a visit if you're ever in that part of France.

To walk among the gravestones, row after row, and to read the names of all the young Canadians who gave their lives to recapture a fallen France from the clutches of a madman called Hitler, will bring your heart to your throat, cause your eyes to water and render you speechless. You might also remember, as we did, that Hitler's initial promise was to liberate the people of Europe, not to enslave them. With that trust he eventually gained the formidable power with which he began to crush not only his own citizens, the Jews, but also his neighbouring countries, one at a time as though they were matchsticks.

As we read the names on the gravestones, we realized that of every three Canadian soldiers who fought and died for the liberation of France, two were English-speaking and the other was French. But they all died side by side as comrades for the very same reason. That reason was to forever make sure that no country or any part of any country should ever again be led down the garden path by some self-proclaimed liberator who, in reality, has nothing more concrete to offer than a mouth full of false hope and a program of experimentation.

What I'm trying to say is this: When we left the cemetery and finally got enough control of ourselves so that we could speak and once again engage in conversation, we immediately focused on the subject of Quebec separation and the dire consequences it would have on all Canadians.

It not only gave us pause to wonder, but it also made us extremely angry at those who would even dare to insult the memory of such fine Canadian examples. After taking two months to tour the highways, byways and back roads of most countries of Europe, and after talking to literally hundreds of the common people, we came to several conclusions that proved to be quite revealing.

1. The country we live in, our form of government, our wide-open spaces, our life-styles and especially our ability to respect and balance our ethnic differences, make us not only the envy of the world, but a people that all other nations can trust.

2. We're an unassuming nation. We don't blow our own horns and we don't flaunt what we've got. This makes people around the world feel comfortable to be around us, whether it's in our country or in theirs.

3. All Canadians, and especially those French Canadians from Quebec who may want to follow their misguided separatist leaders, have absolutely no idea how rich, great and magnificent this country really is. We are

sitting on a gold-mine, and we don't know it. I would like to know how the people of New York State, for example, can manage to have approximately the same standard of living as do most Canadians. Their present population is very close to that of Canada's total, but we live in an area approximately seventy-two times larger than they do. Their natural resources are nearly depleted, while ours have hardly even been touched yet. If you evenly divide our land with its potential hidden wealth among all of us, we would each own eighty-five acres. If you evenly divide New York State's land with its depleted wealth among its citizens, they would each own about one acre. Now, even if 95 percent of our land and wealth is presently inaccessible to each of us, we would still have approximately four times more land with its potential wealth than would our New York counterparts. Wow! I think that anybody who has a stake in this mysterious land of ours would be terribly ill-advised to just pack up, forsake everything and move out, especially at this time when so many people from practically every country in the world would give their eye teeth to move in.

Of course, the separatists claim they will take their land with them when they go. Parizeau has said that if he can get only 50 percent plus one vote, he will take 100 percent of the Quebec people out of Canada. I wouldn't like to speculate on what's going to happen if 49.999 percent of his population decide to stay and keep their land exactly where it is, within the boundaries of Canada. And something tells me that the First Nations of Quebec, with their vast tracts of territory, will be among those wanting to stay.

In wrapping up, I'd like to make one or two more points. The first one pertains to how I feel about this country, why I love it so much and the reason I feel the people of Quebec, if given half a chance, would love it too.

When I stand before the majesty of the snow-capped Rocky Mountains and realize how insignificant I am, the only sound I hear in the silence is my heart pounding out a thunderous message: "As little as I am, these mountains are mine." When I crouch beside a giant Douglas fir and lean over a clear mountain stream and take a drink of its invigorating water, I give thanks too. When I feel the winds from nowhere place a gentle kiss upon my cheek as I gaze upon the pure virginity of our boundless northern territories, I know I must give in to it; I'm in love. Whether it's combines reaping the golden waves or fishing boats riding the blue ones, our children must harvest all Canada's dreams and forever go on dreaming new ones.

I have travelled this country extensively, by foot, car, boat, train and aircraft. Whether I'm playing my guitar in Massey Hall, Toronto, or accompanying an old French fiddler in some little kitchen of an old house in Gaspé, I have known the warmth and sincere hospitality that flows from the hearts of all Canadians everywhere. And even though we may speak different languages, it's our Canadianism that binds us together. That is the quality that makes us unique. That is the trait by which we are identified and recognized throughout the world.

I am just as much a fool if I go to England or Australia and try to convince them that I'm not a Canadian as a Quebecker would be if he went to France and tried to convince them of the same thing. Even if our language didn't give us away, our habits, our manner and our behaviour would. No matter how we try to be other-wise, we are Canadians first. And even though we don't recognize it ourselves, the world does.

I therefore say, first to the Quebeckers who may find themselves on the slippery slope of separatism and then to all Canadians everywhere: Get the hell off your ass and out of your backyards, and instead of flying to Florida to see palm trees, go to the west coast of Canada where the grass is green all winter. They grow palm trees there, too. In the other months, get out and see this great country of ours. Go east, west and north, from ocean to ocean to ocean, and take a deep breath of the air, absorb the scenery, wash yourself in the waters and roll around in the beautiful Canadian dirt. It's yours, you know. It's all yours. And it's even better than that. You are it! And it is you! Inseparable!

The next time you hear the rustle of branches and the flutter of wings, and then discover a small brown nest with two blue eggs, ask yourself, "Did the robins come back to the English? Did the robins come back to the French?" NO! The robins came back to Canada! Go and tell Parizeau to do likewise.

───❧───

Stompin' Tom is a singer-songwriter
and records for
EMI Music (Canada) Ltd.

Standing by
Is Not Enough

———❦———

Peter C. NEWMAN

T HERE was a time, not so long ago, when Hugh MacLennan's adaptation of Rilke's romantic epiphany about "two solitudes" adequately described the benevolent disinterest that characterized French-English relations in this country.

Yet this spring, when Quebec has never been closer to realizing its dream of nationhood and the disintegration of Canada looms as a distinct possibility, we seem to have lapsed from solitude into lassitude. Except for some professional constitutional gun-slingers and the odd Canadian patriot (a breed as rare as witch doctors in modern African documentaries), few in English Canada seem to care what happens to their country or to Quebec. We stand in danger of becoming the only nation in world history to break up out of sheer boredom.

The situation reminds me of a dialogue fragment in one of Arthur Koestler's early novels, in which an exasperated citizen innocent of wrongdoing is being interrogated by a relentless secret service official.

"I accuse this man," intones the prosecutor wearily, "of complicity in murder and crimes of the present, past and future."

"But I never killed a fly," pleads the astonished defendant.

"Ah, but the flies you didn't kill," replies the triumphant official, "brought pestilence to the whole province."

It's a possibility: that what we're *not* doing could cost us our country.

It's because of this very real quandary that I believe standing by is not enough, that we must rally our thoughts and actions in defence of Canada. It won't be easy. There have been too many false alarms—after all,

Confederation was supposed to have caved in when René Lévesque called the referendum in 1980; a decade later, the sun was never supposed to rise again if Meech Lake failed; and two years after that, hell was going to freeze over if Canadians voted to reject the Charlottetown Accord.

While there's no way of knowing whether this time the results might be different, on each of those previous occasions there were passionate voices raised to make the case for a continued partnership. Now, there is only silence. If none of us speak out, *we* deserve to be charged with treason—like that misguided innocent in the Koestler trial—not Jacques Parizeau or Lucien Bouchard, who are dedicated to fighting for *their* country—Quebec.

As of this writing, separatism in Quebec remains a minority cause, but its adherents are buoyed by a vibrant form of politics and a sure sense of place. Since most English Canadians have no personal framework within which to fit or even understand that kind of impulse for self-determination, they tend to interpret each of the Parti or Bloc Québécois's policy declamations as the hot breath of revolution.

The dialogue then becomes not, how do we get to like or even tolerate each other again, but what value can we place on staying together, how useful can we be to each other within a continuing Canadian alliance?

For starters, that means English Canada must give up the silly notion that the status quo remains a viable option. It's not, and we mustn't keep pretending that not discussing alternatives makes it so.

At the same time, moderate Quebeckers must begin to realize that their historical notion of Canada as a marriage of convenience between two distinct societies is dead, if it was ever alive. When Toronto, which is the capital of non-French Canada, is populated by less than

40 percent of what used to be called WASPs, you know there's a new country out there and that those porridge-eating, pale-skinned conciliators with Scottish names and mid-Atlantic accents aren't in charge any more. That doesn't make so-called English Canada any less interesting or less worthwhile—on the contrary—but it does mean that there's a new reality in play, which most Quebeckers have so far ignored. And what they've not taken into account is that this new coalition has roots, just as strong if not as deep, in their society as French Canadians have in theirs.

Messieurs Bouchard and Parizeau are intelligent and suave ambassadors for their cause but they are also true believers, and some of their revolutionary ideas are strictly Looney Tunes. Their basic tactical and strategic error is to believe that Canadians outside Quebec will accept the splitting asunder of their country with cool equanimity.

It's not going to happen. In this modern age, you don't need too many people at the barricades to make the point to the world (especially the international currency traders) that Quebec's future as an independent state will not be financed by a Canada deprived of its historic roots and ocean-to-ocean geography. Canadians love their country as much as Bouchard and Parizeau love their would-be republic. Quebec independence will not be achieved without a horrendously traumatic period of adjustment. The most likely victims of that transition— at least in terms of lower living standards—will be citizens of Quebec, the very people who imagine that sovereignty will resolve the economic issues it will create.

In his many speeches and interviews, Lucien Bouchard, that courageous but misguided symbol of sovereignty, keeps stressing that "Canada will have the same reasons as Quebec for maintaining the present rules relating to the free circulation of people, goods, services and capital. Good sense will prevail during these discussions. Already holding a quarter of the Canadian supply, a sovereign Quebec will support the maintenance of a monetary union as an important guarantee of economic stability."

It ain't necessarily so. No province of any state anywhere that has split away from its mother country has been able to maintain use of the stronger currency of its original nationality. For example, not a single one of the many republics that once made up the U.S.S.R. uses the ruble as its official currency, even though they all want it. It is nothing less than political fraud for Bouchard and Parizeau to pretend, as they do, that if Quebec separates it can keep everything it has now, as well as gain the benefits of political independence.

At nearly every press conference, the leader of the Parti Québécois reiterates his curious position of coming out simultaneously for virginity and motherhood. "Let's keep things as they are," he snorts through his moustache. "As soon as Quebec becomes sovereign, I don't want fast economic and commercial negotiations with the rest of Canada." As well as affirming that Quebec would retain the Canadian dollar as its currency ("to maintain the economic status quo between Quebec and Canada"), Parizeau goes on to suggest that such potentially controversial issues as division of the national debt (and presumably the status of the First Nations within a newly independent Quebec) should be left until "after the political situation has calmed." In other words, Quebec will claim its independence from a supine Canada led by a spineless Ottawa that allows the most tricky negotiating points to be set over for discussion to some ill-defined future.

I think not.

The last time separatism in Quebec became such an ugly issue was under the late René Lévesque, who in 1980 called—and lost—a referendum on sovereignty-association. That hybrid term signified anything anybody wanted it to mean, even in a country like Canada, which once oxymoronically billed itself as "a self-governing colony." The only historic precedent to "sovereignty-association" was the madcap constitution of the Austro-Hungarian empire. The late Eugene Forsey, a lapsed socialist who was appointed to the Senate by Pierre Trudeau and who knew more about the Canadian constitution than anyone else, including his sponsor, once described sovereignty-association as "a horse that won't start, let alone run. You can no more negotiate sovereignty-association than you can negotiate sour sugar, dry water, boiling ice or stationary motion."

The substance of Forsey's argument hasn't changed, even though the PQ/BQ position often smells like a glorified version of "sovereignty-association." The Bouchard/Parizeau image of themselves embarking upon this pure and beautiful mission of shedding the Canada that has held Quebec in its constitutional chains for 128 years—yet wanting to keep all the good things about their tormentor—makes no more sense now than it did in 1980.

We're either one nation or two. Period.

In this context, it's one of the supreme ironies of the Quebec *indépendantiste* movement that its leaders intend to finance the break-up of Canada using Canadian dollars. That's too much—as the country and western ditties have it—like being your own grandpaw.

During his western tour last year, Bouchard was very specific: "We already have 24 percent of the Canadian currency circulating, and we'll keep it," he told anyone who would listen. "That's our money and we'll use it. Nobody would want to see Quebeckers dumping $24 billion on the market—it would be a terrible blow to the currency."

Even if English Canadians were mutton-headed enough to consider sharing their currency with the newly created political entity that had destroyed their future as a country, it is quite simply impossible for two major sovereign states to have a single currency. Several countries (mainly Panama and Liberia) use the American dollar as official tender, but their balance of payments positions are so dismal that no functioning monetary union actually exists. Similarly, the nine former French colonies that combined their monetary destinies by forming the West African Monetary Union have since had to impose severe foreign exchange controls to prevent capital flights. The world's only functioning monetary union is the partnership between Belgium and Luxembourg, but the tiny grand-duchy's population is only 4 percent of Belgium's, and since it regularly runs budget surpluses, the postage-stamp country has felt little policy restraint. The great experiment in forging a monetary union has of course been the attempt to negotiate use of a common currency within the European Union. Paradoxically, those negotiations prove why Quebec and Canada couldn't follow its example. Monetary union generally forces member countries to move towards a high degree of political integration.

The Maastricht Treaty of December 1991, which set down the matrix for monetary union, also made it very clear that this would mean loss of not only monetary but fiscal autonomy for its dozen member states. That's why the treaty's approval has had such a rough ride in Denmark, the United Kingdom and Germany. If the partners implement the dramatic pact, the end result will be a political, economic and sociological European union not that different from Canadian Confederation. That's what Canada has now, so it hardly seems worthwhile for Quebec to separate while insisting on a common currency. The ultimate consequence of maintaining a joint dollar would mean evolving into a new Canada that operated much like the old one. Why bother?

Not only do Canada's ten provinces form a functioning (if far from perfect) economic partnership but existing trade flows document that Quebec sells more of its products to the rest of Canada than it does to the balance of the world. Canadians left behind in a split-apart country would not likely place much emphasis on perpetuating that access. At the same time, the new Bouchard/Parizeau republic would not necessarily gain access to the North American Free Trade area—especially since Canada holds veto power over the admission of new members.

"Simply put," stated a Royal Bank study published in 1992, "there is no realistic possibility of two truly sovereign states sharing the same currency while exercising independent control over the monetary, fiscal and other economic policies that underpin that currency. A nation's currency is one of the most basis expressions of its existence. If two countries share the same monetary, fiscal and other essential government policies, then neither country is truly independent."

Because both territories would be severely weakened by separation, the resultant dramatic jump in interest rates—with all the damage that would inflict on consumer and corporate buying patterns—would significantly weaken two already fragile economies. There would, at least in the initial stages, not be sufficient funds flowing into the country to pay the annual $55 billion or more in interest on Canada's national debt, no matter how it's divided. That would set off a high-risk foreign exchange crisis that would almost inevitably attract the International Monetary Fund's emergency measures squad. Pension funds would be among the hardest hit, but every aspect of Canadian and Quebec life would suffer. Living standards would drop at least 15 percent, personal incomes would plummet by about $10,140 per family and unemployment would rise to 15 percent or more. Canada would become Newfoundland writ large.

Sensing the loss of opportunity, at least a million Canadians would emigrate to the United States. As is always the case in such an economically inspired exodus, we would lose our best and brightest.

The loopiest of Jacques Parizeau's ideas is his current plan to base his independence strategy squarely on the tactics used earlier this year by Rogers Cable Ltd. to force its viewers to pay for the new Canadian specialty channels. Instead of allowing Quebec's citizens to decide openly whether they support separation, the PQ leader explained that the National Assembly would pass an edict unilaterally declaring Quebec a sovereign country. Only as an afterthought would voters be allowed to express their feelings about what, by then, would be a done deal. This is an exact copy of Ted Rogers's negative-option marketing plan, and one hopes that the dismal fate of the latter will be repeated in the dismissal of the former.

A desperate ploy by a bush-league Machiavelli, the Parizeau gambit was not, as many commentators claimed at the time, too clever by half. It was too stupid by half, because if there is one thing Quebeckers have demonstrated over and over again, it's their collective wisdom of voting in their highest self-interest. So far, the leaders of the PQ and BQ have not been able to demonstrate a single advantage of nationhood to the *people*—as opposed to the politicians—of Quebec. Not only will an independent Quebec keep the Canadian dollar *and* Canadian passports, Parizeau has promised, but the newly independent republic will belong to the Commonwealth and will join NATO and NAFTA. (It will, presumably, encourage its citizens to curse Ottawa and make fun of Toronto. Hell, that's what being Canadian is all about.)

The Parizeau logic would have us believe that transition to independence would be so smooth that hardly anyone would notice. The only real change, one assumes, would be in his own status. Instead of being the lowly premier of an important province, he would become the exalted president of a marginal republic, able to bore United Nations assemblies with his avuncular lectures and fly the *fleur-de-lis* from the fender of his limousine. He would at last be officially installed in his Quebec City presidential palace, instead of merely living in a donated house that looks like one.

None of Parizeau's calming homilies ring true. If Quebec were to become independent after the referendum, everything would change. The Canada we know and love would vanish as a viable state. Our geography, outrageous to begin with but held together by its coast-to-coast-to-coast dimensions, would become unmanageable. The gaping hole where Quebec once flourished would tear the country into many pieces. The means used by Quebec to leave Confederation would have to be made available to the other provinces. British Columbia and Alberta, together or apart, would soon follow, becoming either Pacific Rim principalities or northern extensions of the new Cascadia, already forming on the Pacific coast.

The main problem for those of us who care about this country is that the federalist side lacks leaders. Ottawa's tactics are either dumb or naive; certainly they're grossly inadequate. Jean Chrétien's hands-off policy reminds me of a Robin Williams sketch in which he parodies Britain's traditionally unarmed constables. Faced by an escaping bank robber, the policeman shouts, "Stop!" Nothing happens. The thief keeps running. "If you don't halt immediately," comes the warning from the law, "I'll shout 'STOP!' again!"

This seems to be the beginning and end of Jean Chrétien's strategy. "For Quebec to separate from Canada would be completely illegal and unconstitutional," he keeps repeating, like some mountain dweller's mantra. He's right, of course, but the world works according to different rules. It's not easy to find a country that in recent times has separated from its former motherland by strict legal and constitutional means. Countries get born through revolutions or some charismatic leader declaring to the world community: "Hey, guess what? We've just become a country! Let's party."

At the moment, a hardening of English Canada's attitudes towards Quebec threatens both our futures. Certainly in the western provinces, the rules of the game have changed. The mood of most people, as far as one can determine their feelings, parallels the attitude towards Quebec championed by Preston Manning and his Reformers: indifference bordering on hostility. Even those who in the past have supported French Canada's aspirations and did their best to support national unity by dipping their kids in French immersion courses now say flat out that they will not allow Quebec to destroy Confederation. The mood is harsh and uncompromising, reminiscent of the old Chicago blues song, "I told you I love you—now get out!"

Canada's constitutional optimists have always comforted themselves with the notion that this country takes a lot of killing.

This time around, we may have to test that questionable aphorism to its limits.

Peter C. Newman's new book,
The Canadian Revolution:
From Compliance to Defiance,
will be published this fall by Viking.

A Country
for Our Children

❦

Judy MAPPIN

THIS is being written on a winter's day in Ste-Adèle-en-Haut, one hour's drive north of Montreal in the Laurentian mountains. It has been an ideal February day with the snow crisp and white and glistening in the sunshine. There are goldfinches and chickadees at our feeder, and not far away, a porcupine has been sighted pulling the bark off the trees. Conditions are just right for cross-country skiing. On the trails, passing skiers greet one another with "*bon jour*" regardless of which language is their first. In the village of Ste-Adèle, in the stores where we shop, we speak in French and are usually answered in French, but occasionally we are spoken to in English in a good-natured manner. The young man at the service station where we fill up the car is proud of his nearly impeccable English.

At the same time, throughout Quebec, Jacques Parizeau's travelling circus is swinging through the province, purportedly seeking submissions from people both for and against "sovereignty" (i.e., separation) but, in reality, pushing its cause, which is to destroy Canada. Those who speak for Canada are sometimes listened to politely but at other times are treated with derision by the commissioners and the audience. I have heard people phoning into a local talk show saying that they are for Canada but are afraid to speak in front of the commissions because of the reaction of their bosses and fellow workers. And this in a free country! What a tragic situation! And sometimes it seems that those who get up to speak do not stick to the agenda but bring up their own worries—unemployment, daycare and the like—which are of more concern to them than whether Quebec should separate.

My husband, an English-speaking Quebecker, was born in this province and has always lived here. He has contributed to the Quebec community all his working life. It is his home and his right to be here. I have lived here for over forty years. This is my home. We don't want to live anywhere else. But we are Canadians and will never give up our Canadian passports.

In 1974, I opened, with two partners, a bookstore selling only books by Canadians. We felt then and do now that we were and are making a positive statement about the quality of the work of Canadian writers, and we wanted to make their books more easily available. Most of our books are in English for there are many fine bookstores in Montreal selling books in French. We carry translations of French-language books written by Quebeckers and other Canadians who write in French. Our French-speaking customers come to the store to buy books written by English-speaking Canadians, and sometimes poets and others come in and peruse our shelves looking for poetry and fiction that they would like to see translated into French. In our twenty years of business, we have seen this last activity increase and have sensed a dialogue developing between writers of both languages. If Quebec separates, I wonder what will happen to the bridges that have been built. I know I will not have the incentive to carry on.

It is nonsense to say that Canadians have no identity and equally ridiculous to say that there is not a Canadian culture. Just come into my bookstore. I will show you our identity expressed by our writers. Or watch a film made by Canadians, experience their dance and their music, see the work of our artists or watch the youngsters playing a game of pick-up hockey or singing around a camp-fire or paddling on our lakes at summer camp.

I am troubled and afraid. I'm not so much afraid for my husband and myself. We have lived most of our lives; we can stay or go where we want. But I am afraid for my children wherever they are in Canada and for my grandchildren, and for other people's children whatever their first language. If Quebec separates, I fear they will not have a country. And I am afraid for the children of French-speaking Quebeckers who are not being taught in their schools to speak English; whatever happens, their lives will be severely restricted. In most parts of the country, parents of English-speaking children can choose to have them educated in French immersion classes.

We are lucky. Our children have the opportunity to grow up speaking two of the most widely used languages in the world. European children grow up speaking several languages as a matter of course, and some here make so much fuss about two!

It is tragic that a handful of intellectuals and politicians with their own agenda are attempting, often aided and abetted by the media, to manipulate Quebeckers into believing they will be better off in a "sovereign" Quebec.

It is also tragic that so much of the time and energy of our leaders and of ordinary people are taken up with the referendum debate when Canada, said to be the best country in the world in which to live, is burdened with tremendous problems: the poor and homeless, those who seek jobs and cannot find them, our debt that almost puts us in the category of a third-world country, our horrendous sales of weapons to countries that we know to be abusing human rights, and our environmental concerns. These and other serious matters have to be addressed *now*, and yet the referendum to come is dominating every action and decision.

There have been times when I have felt that the rest of Canada scarcely acknowledges the fact that there are English-speaking Quebeckers with a long history in the building of this province. However, now that the crisis long anticipated is imminent, I am heartened that the fact I have been asked to write this essay means that we do count. One of my friends in Ontario recently expressed the feeling shared by many Canadians outside of Quebec—that she ought to have a say in what happens to our country.

The first immigrants to Canada were our native peoples. Then came the French and the English, who fought and then, later on, founded together the modern Canada. Since then, there have been waves of immigrants from all over the world. They came here to be Canadians.

It is only thirty years ago that Canada acquired a flag of its own. Its design symbolizes our motto, "A Mari Usque Ad Mare," from sea to sea, not only from the Atlantic to the Pacific, but also from the northern lands and waters to the longest friendly border in the world. Quebeckers, I believe, are a sensible people. I am hopeful that in the privacy of the ballot box they will overwhelmingly vote for Canada, which is, to quote the Right Honourable Joe Clark, "a nation too good to lose."

⚜

Judy Mappin was born in Toronto;
graduated in Science from McGill University;
has been a Quebecker for more than
forty years; and is a wife, mother,
grandmother and bookseller.

Canada: Building on Success

Matthew W. BARRETT

EW countries anywhere can match the range of strengths that Canada possesses. We have growing strength in the export of value-added manufactured goods. We are showing world-class prowess in computer software and telecommunications and in other areas—all of which translates into highly skilled, highly paid, knowledge-based jobs. We are no longer simple importers of ready-made and all-too-often outdated technology. Rather we use our own skills to build on our own technology and that of others, and re-export it enhanced.

Canada is displaying these skills at a time when both our traditional and our emerging markets are more open than they have ever been before. We can expect growing opportunities for Canadian exporters as a result of the NAFTA agreement (which Chile has been invited to join), from the Uruguay Round of the General Agreement on Tariffs and Trade, under which barriers will fall to a greater degree than ever before, and from our membership in Asia Pacific Economic Cooperation, the APEC organization that links us to the dynamic nations of east Asia and the Pacific. It's critically important to realize that *all* Canadians, from sea to sea, are in an outstanding position to seize the market opportunities opening up in the Asia-Pacific region and in many other parts of the world. Canada's unique position as a full-fledged member of both an expanding NAFTA and APEC, combined with the gigantic U.S. market on our doorstep, present stunning opportunities for us to capitalize on Canada's strengths.

Thus for Canadians, the transformation of the world economy is not a threat. It is an unmatched opportunity. And it is an opportunity we are especially well placed to grasp. The "Made in Canada" label is welcome everywhere, not only because of our product or service quality, but because of the respect in which the name of Canada is held for our contribution to peace and world order, and our record as a country of democracy, decency, civility and social justice. Don't underestimate the competitive advantage every Canadian exporter derives from this storehouse of positive goodwill. I see it wherever I go on behalf of the Bank of Montreal.

Canada is opening these new doors abroad because of the most significant change of all, an *attitudinal* change. Canadian business has become far more externally oriented. We were always a trading nation, of course, but it has been well said that we were not necessarily a nation of traders. In contrast, today, every single business person I speak to is travelling around the world to find out who is best, who is leading and what has to be done to compete with the leaders. Canada is already becoming a nation of formidable traders, and in the markets of the world that "Made in Canada" label shows our flag on more and more finished goods, and on more and more of the *ideas* that add value to goods.

This change in mindset has also been evident right at home. Since the mid-1980s we've been laying many of the foundations for a lasting improvement in our overall economic performance. We've kept inflation at rates that make us the envy of the world. The federal government has introduced major structural changes in the economy, the successful pursuit of trade agreements among them. The business sector has been sharpening its competitive edge, adopting advanced technology and undergoing profound restructuring.

Perhaps the most striking shift in attitude is the way in which we Canadians are creating new partnerships among ourselves. To compete successfully in global markets, a country like ours, with a small population and vast geography, must have unique levels of co-operation among all sectors of society. Today, business, government, labour and universities are all working together on numerous fronts to ensure that Canadians meet the challenges of international competition.

Canada *is* working. Consider the evidence.

In the third quarter of 1994, our overall economic growth output grew at a year-over-year rate of 4.8 percent. We did better than all the other leading industrial nations that make up the G7. And the OECD has predicted that we will lead the G7 in growth, both this year and in 1996.

Canadian exporters, of course, played a crucially important part in this success story. Exports to the United States have risen by almost 65 percent since 1991. Merchandise trade overall is booming, with our annualized surplus running at $21 billion in October 1994. Exports of goods and services are at an all-time high, both in absolute dollars and as a percentage of GDP. In fact, we lead the G7 nations in the relative value of our exports to our output, and in the third quarter of 1994 our exports of real goods and services reached an astonishing 38.1 percent of GDP—up from 26 percent in the 1980s.

As a result of our economic achievements last year, employment is up by nearly 2 percent. In 1994 Canada created 341,000 jobs, all of them in the private sector, and what is especially encouraging, all of them were full-time. That was the best figure since 1987—the best figure in seven years—and as a result, unemployment, while still too high, *has fallen*, and has fallen to 9.6 percent.

That's how the combination of enlightened trade agreements, Canada's high international status, an externally directed outlook and a new spirit of co-operation within the country have enabled us to build on our fundamental strengths. Indeed, evidence abounds that we in Canada—the public and private sectors working together—*do* have the ability to meet international competition, keep the jobs we have and create the new jobs this country badly needs.

Yet two major issues face us. Both must be answered in the near term. And *how* we answer them, will, in large measure, decide whether we can go on building on this remarkable success.

First, we urgently need action to deal with Canada's debt and deficit problem. The decisions Canada makes regarding debt and deficits are absolutely crucial to our future well-being as a nation. Our growing indebtedness is a virus that is already debilitating us. Failure to take effective, timely action will undermine those economic strengths I have just described.

Yet here too, there is reason today for much more optimism than we might have felt only two years ago. A broad consensus has emerged among Canadians everywhere that the growth of our debts must be halted and reversed, and that our only rational and politically acceptable option is to cut the level of public spending. Governments across Canada are making increasingly successful efforts to do exactly that, and the federal government, in the budget brought down in late February, has presented some initial proposals in the same vein.

Critical though our public finances are, our political future is even more important. Canadians in all provinces need to ask themselves, "Has federalism worked? Has being a member of this federation, as it stands today, added to our prosperity, our freedom, our quality of life?" We all need to ask those questions and reflect on them, because our answer will determine our attitude towards the referendum in Quebec, as well as our attitude towards making any adjustments that may be required in future.

I think the evidence I have just outlined suggests very strongly that Canadian federalism *has* worked, that it has worked outstandingly well and that it can do even more for us in future. Canada is the envy of the world, which is why so many people are knocking at our door. The United Nations recognizes our achievements, too, and has ranked Canada number one. This fact has been cited frequently, and it should be; we need to be reminded often that we have built a very successful country on the northern half of this continent, and that the world recognizes it, even if we sometimes don't.

We often talk of this country as if we were uniquely disadvantaged, having to deal with diversity. But one brief look around the world would surely show that Canada is among the most fortunate of nations. Name one country on this planet that isn't debating adjustments to its constitutional and/or political and/or social institutional arrangements. Name one that isn't struggling to redefine internal arrangements and its relationship with the world. Name one. I can't.

Of course no country has built Utopia, and Canada is far from doing so. But our difficulties, important and fundamental as they are, by world standards are eminently manageable. In the real world, the life of every country is a journey, a work-in-progress. There is no once-and-for-all solution, no silver bullet. Countries must continuously re-shape themselves, adapting to the changing world around them. So it has been for us. The key reason that Canada has been so successful is that from 1867 to this day, we have been adjusting our federalism to changing needs and changing times. We shall go on doing that. Let's not let political frustration drive us into misguided or precipitous actions.

Canadian unity has been integral to our national success. For Canada the loss of Quebec would be a terrible self-inflicted wound. It would be the dismantling of a powerful national entity and the break-up of a family whose roots go back more than two hundred years. We

If You Love This Country

have a shared history. We have built a great country together, indeed one of the universal success stories. In a world beset by tensions and rivalries, Canada's achievement stands out as a beacon of moderation and accommodation. We owe it to ourselves, we owe it to succeeding generations—not to mention the world community—to ensure that our federation endures. And each of us has a part in preserving Canada.

I believe the people of Quebec will opt for Canada. I believe that Canadians everywhere will reach out to Quebec and keep our country united, for practical reasons and also from a deep national pride. All Canadians can influence the outcome by our attitudes, our traditional civility and moderation, our sense of great things done together and greater things yet to do. I have supreme confidence in the wisdom of the people of Quebec. I have supreme confidence in the wisdom of all Canadians.

Matthew Barrett joined the Bank of Montreal thirty-two years ago as a clerk in London, England, and was appointed Chairman of the Board and Chief Executive Officer in 1990.

Pieces
of Sky

❧

Neil BISSOONDATH

We are what the geography of the country has made us…. That is why we are, in a sense, nearer to English Canadians than to Frenchmen.
After a month in Paris, which I loved with all my heart, I just the same got very lonesome for our trees, and the sight of the Laurentides and the horizon of Quebec. I felt lonesome for the Canadian sky so vast and so grandiose.
In Paris, you have pieces of sky.

Roger Lemelin, Quebec novelist,
from a letter written in English, 1950.

IT has become popular in recent years for many, in both public and private life, to insist that there are no such things as Canadian values and, by extension, a Canadian culture. This is a peculiar notion in a country that has existed as a political entity for almost 130 years and as a historical one for even longer. It is a way of saying that Canada and Canadians have no reality.

But the nation, fractious and uneasy as it frequently is, *does* exist, and so do its values. They may not always be readily identifiable, they may not always be easily defined, but their effect can be sniffed in the very air that surrounds us. Canada may physically resemble the United States in many ways, but when I cross the border I know immediately that I am in a foreign land. The psychic electricity is different, alien. It tells me that I am no longer at home.

Principles, values and beliefs—words used by Pierre Elliott Trudeau in a statement of affirmative values attached to the Charter of Rights and Freedoms—are the playthings of moral philosophers and theologians, the rallying cries of religious fundamentalists, the linguistic torches of politicians seeking a tone of higher order. They have also become concepts of battle plans in a Canada profoundly shaped by the ideas of Pierre Trudeau.

They say there was a time when you could tell the Canadian easily; he was the one who would stuff empty candy wrappers and gnawed apple cores into his pockets until he came to a garbage can. Then he'd stand there as if in holy communion, muttering phrases that ended with "…eh?" and making offerings at the altar of civic pride.

We have always defined our pride differently. But this particular trait was set on the path to a slow death by the advent some years ago of the word "biodegradable." Silently assuring ourselves that nature would take care of it, Canadians began acquiring new abilities: surreptitious flicks of the wrist and—"Nice lookin' clouds up there, eh?"—eyes that wandered resolutely away from the flight paths of balled paper or empty cigarette packs. Today, the Canadian litters with the best of them. Specificity, it must be said, may be dwindling.

And yet, they say, the Canadian continues to reveal himself most readily in other ways, with an overheated politeness, for instance: Tread accidentally on a Canadian's foot, and *he* falls all over himself apologizing to *you*. Many view this as a silly trait. I do not. In some parts of the world, you'd be lucky to get away with just a scowl. In other parts of the world, you'd be lucky to get away with your life. The Canadian's urge to apologize for having got his shoe under yours strikes me as endearing and eminently civilized.

We cannot trust stereotype, of course. The best it can offer is general direction. But this part of the Canadian stereotype is, I hope, true. For it suggests the principles, values and beliefs that define the character of a people shaped by a particular history.

So just what, at this time in our history, are Canadian values?

This is a question usually posed by those who would deny their existence. Instead, the very asking of the question often tends to be an attempt to belittle the notion itself, as if the identification of a value as Canadian is somehow meant to deny it to others. But of course this is not so.

I suspect we glimpsed one such value in the thousands of get-well messages Bloc Québécois leader Lucien Bouchard received from Canadians outside Quebec during his life-threatening illness: to abhor the man's political dream is not necessarily to abhor the man. Values such as this—the recognition that the human being is worth more than political principle—lend texture to a society. It will be argued that such an attitude is not exclusive to Canada, and that is true. But it is not common to *all* societies, and I would suggest that its being shared by others does not make it less Canadian.

A glimpse of the land before history.

A blazing camp-fire late at night, beneath a sky luminous with more stars than the mind could comfortably conjure: nature's way, you think, of dwarfing the human imagination, not into insignificance but into a proper perspective of its place in the larger world. Like the prairie sky, perhaps, or the reach of the Rockies, which have a way of dampening arrogance, of imposing a vital modesty.

Way up there, in a sky so large it defies the mind to go beyond cliché, a single tiny light cuts a rapid course through the glittering darkness, the satellite's path somehow deepening the silence that is already as profound, as all-encompassing, as that of the world before time. You feel yourself alone despite the companionship of neighbouring camp-fires lit by people—anglophone, francophone—who offer little more than a smile, a nod, a wave: no more is required, no more expected. The communality of purpose is sufficient. The experience we are sharing goes beyond words or invitations or the usual requirements of social convention.

It was the writer Margaret Visser who pointed out to me that camping—this safest of engagements with the natural world—can justly be viewed as a Canadian ritual. And ritual, let us remember, is the physical representation of values. To sit there, then, between camp-fire and tent, in the utter safety of a national park, is to feel the self part of a larger, miraculous whole. It is to immerse yourself, however fleetingly, in the power of a social value rarely seen as such: to understand the modesty for which Canadians are justly known.

It was Canadian prime minister John Diefenbaker who, in protest against apartheid at the 1961 Commonwealth Conference, arranged the expulsion of South Africa from the organization. And it was Prime Minister Brian Mulroney who, many years later at another Commonwealth conference, earned the enmity of British prime minister Margaret Thatcher by leading the battle for the imposition of severe trade sanctions against the government in Pretoria.

The battle against racism by Canadians may be imperfect—here at home, for instance, discomfort can be found in attitudes towards blacks and Asians, and in conditions on numerous Native reserves—but it has been many decades since the principle of racial segregation has found any public favour in this country. Individuals continue to struggle with their own racism, trying to bridge the chasm between the heart—which has been taught racial distrust—and the mind, which has recognized the evil of it.

And yet....

Even as apartheid slides steadily into the history books, even as South Africa under the leadership of Nelson Mandela struggles to achieve a society free of racial segregation, we here in Canada are seeing it take root—in the name of equality. In Ontario, demands are made for the public funding of segregated schools. In British Columbia, a Chinese parents' association is set up. The Writers' Union of Canada funds a racially segregated conference, and governments across the country implement hiring policies based partly on race. The list can go on to disheartening lengths.

A queer thing is happening, then, to this value so long cherished. It is not so much slipping away as metamorphosing into an ugly version of itself, acquiring the justification that the founders of apartheid once used for that abhorrent system: that, somehow, separate could also mean equal. Values are not static things. They evolve as society evolves. They come and they go. But it seems to me that some values are worth holding on to, and a value that dreams of a society based not on racial difference but on racial equality is among the most important.

The founder of the Chinese Parents' Association in Richmond, British Columbia, recently said to an interviewer, "What is a Canadian value? Can somebody define to me what's a Canadian value?" If you begin with the assumption that Canadian values do not exist, then you remain blind to this anti-racism value that has driven Canadian political and private principles for many years. And you remain equally blind to the implications of your own attitudes.

The difference between innocence and naïvety is not always clear, yet the former can be seen as a positive trait—as in the innocence of children—while the second is reviled as being a small step away from stupidity. Innocence implies having a trusting nature, while naïvety implies simplemindedness.

And so I opt for the word "innocence" to describe what seems to constitute an enduring, and laudable, Canadian quality. Indeed, so ingrained is it that I would go so far as to call it a Canadian *value*.

Consider, for instance, the public outrage that met the broadcast of videotapes from the Canadian Airborne Regiment. What those tapes offered were the antics of brutes who happened to be Canadian. To anyone who has seen Gwynne Dyer's superb documentary series "War," the behaviour on our television screens was distressing but hardly surprising.

We found it distressing because this is not how we see ourselves. We believe in our own clean-cut, good-guy image. And even if we know that the military does not aim to create Boy Scouts, even if we know that the ultimate goal of military training is to produce efficient killers, we still want them to reflect our image of ourselves: we want our killers clean-cut, polite and well-behaved.

It was suggested to me at the time that the outrage merely revealed the profound naïvety of the Canadian public. On reflection, I agreed, but suggested the word "innocence" instead. I did not see this as condemnation. Instead, I thought it a becoming innocence, heartening proof of how seriously we take our notions of goodness. I saw it as a confirmation of idealism.

Five or six years ago, my companion and I were on vacation in France. Wandering around Nice one morning, we spotted on a deserted street two 500-franc notes (about $250 in all), one lying on the sidewalk, the other under a parked car. With visions of some frantic pensioner in our heads, we entered a nearby bank in the hopes that a customer may have reported their loss.

We were met with utter incredulity. No, no one had reported losing money. We could go to the police with it, but why do that? If the money went unclaimed, it would be ours—but we were tourists, we'd be long gone by the time the waiting period expired.... Implicit in the tone was *Mais voyons donc*, don't be silly: As we stood there, the bills held uneasily in our hands, they asked where we were from, and on being told, mumbled, "Ahh, les gentils canadiens....", in a way that said judgements were being made, conclusions being drawn. The touch of condescension was unmistakable: as if they were big-city sophisticates instructing their naïve brethren in the ways of the world. You knew that stories would be told of the innocent Canadians, that we would be objects of mirth. And yet, for once, condescension did not rankle. After all, in the larger scheme of things it was not a bad image to leave behind.

We took our leave, feeling a little silly, a little guilty— and, as far as I was concerned, glad to be an innocent Canadian in a world that saw naïvety in simple honesty.

Innocence, naïvety: call it what you will. But to give up on it is to surrender our essential idealism. We seem at times to be in danger of doing just that. The signs are there: in those, for instance, who would break Quebec away from Canada as well as in those who, through weariness or short-sightedness, would allow Quebec to break away from Canada; in a growing willingness to sacrifice the unfortunate of our society in the name of fiscal responsibility; and in marvelling at the multiplicity of languages on European cereal boxes while raging at the other official language printed on our own.

Principles, values and beliefs are big words easily tossed around. Politicians and philosophers believe they give them weight, but they rarely ever do; they merely make evident the weight with which they have already been invested by the public at large. And it is our little actions that give them weight, lend them meaning: that give us as a people, anglophone and francophone, a specific personality that is not always easily perceived but that is there nonetheless, shaping us and being shaped by us in an act of mutual and ongoing creation.

Canada has always been an act of faith—and acts of faith depend on idealism. To give up on our innocence is to give up on our idealism, is to give up on ourselves. It is to astigmatize our eyes so that what we see is not the whole sky but just pieces of it.

Neil Bissoondath is a Canadian novelist.

Canada—
Death By
Indifference?

Lewis W. MacKenzie,
MSC, CD
Major-General (ret'd)

IT was the fifth of August 1992, in the morning. As I scanned the front page of the Ottawa paper, I felt an overwhelming surge of emotion; inexplicably, my eyes filled with tears and the headlines blurred. I panicked and turned down a side-street that would take me away from the morning pedestrian rush-hour traffic and back to my home in the Glebe.

It wasn't until I got home some five minutes later and scanned the paper's front page for the second time that I understood the cause of my emotional response.

I had returned to Ottawa late the previous night, the final stage in a journey that had started in Sarajevo three days earlier. For five months I had watched a country self-destruct before my very eyes. Four of the Yugoslavian equivalent to our provinces had unilaterally declared their independence. Having done so over the objection of some of their significant minorities, neighbours started killing neighbours in an attempt to carve out even smaller "ethnically pure" subdivisions of territory, all of this in a country previously envied for its ethnic tolerance. If it could happen in Yugoslavia, the odds were pretty good that it could happen just about anywhere.

Having lived with the butchery of a civil war and all its attendant misery for the thousands of innocent victims, I was shocked to find the front page of a prominent Canadian newspaper filled with the whining and agonizing of a complacent and relatively comfortable population: the GST, the underground economy, strikes, postal rates, lousy weather predicted for the weekend, etc., etc., *ad nauseam.*

Now, I grant you, to GST or not to GST was pretty important stuff in Canada at the time but compared to a mother in Sarajevo seeing her daughter shot through the head by a sniper while on her way to a makeshift school, it seemed more than a little innocuous and hardly worthy of front-page treatment in the capital of a nation that has so much to offer to the international community.

When any nation in the world has a serious security problem and must endure the humiliation of asking outsiders for help, it normally turns to the United Nations for assistance. The UN, in turn, usually gives the troubled nation some say in deciding which countries will provide the military forces to come over its borders wearing the blue beret.

With 185 nations represented in the UN, a nation in crisis has a lot of choices when it comes to recommending which foreign armies it would like to see manning positions on its sovereign territory. At the end of the evaluation process, Canada is always on the list of acceptable/desirable countries to contribute peace-keeping forces for a number of reasons:

- No territorial ambitions. We can't even look after what we have to our satisfaction so the last thing we need is more territory!

- No colonial past (other than being two colonies ourselves). We have never gone abroad with our flag, jabbed it in the ground and declared someone else's territory our own.

- Even-handed foreign aid and policy. Although constantly criticized at home, when observed from abroad, which I did for some fifteen years, Canada is seen as a fair and compassionate country. We never humiliate people or countries when we give them help. Many nations stand on a soap-box and proclaim their generosity when they assist others. Not Canada—figuratively we slide our contribution under the table and whisper, "Take it—it's from Canada." It's a wonderful characteristic.

- Tolerance. Believe it or not, we are a tolerant nation. In fact, we are arguably the most tolerant nation in the world; however, because of our obsession with being perfect, we are much too hard on ourselves when it comes to measuring our achievement in an intolerant world.

- Outstanding soldiers. There is not another nation in the world that can match Canada's exemplary reputation in peace-keeping and coalition operations in support of the UN. Forty-eight years of unblemished international service was not eclipsed in any way by one tragic event in Somalia in 1992. During my three visits to Belet Huen in 1992 and 1994, the local leadership, police and even the father of the murdered Somalia youth pleaded for the Canadians to stay in 1992 and return in 1994. This contribution to the world is not without cost. One hundred Canadian servicemen have given their lives in the service of peace.

When all of the above factors are taken into consideration, Canada always comes out at, or close to, the top of desirable nations to help others. It's not that those in need love us, like us or, in some cases, even respect us, but, in comparison with the other 184 countries in the United Nations, we are the most sought-after when it comes to putting a peace-keeping force together. It is both a curse and a blessing, but we should take pride in why it happens and think very seriously before we reduce our commitment to the UN. Peace-keeping, more than any other policy, is how we export our values abroad for others to see and evaluate.

The Canadian soldiers who do that peace-keeping, in

ever increasing numbers, in some of the most dangerous locations around the world, are a microcosm of Canada abroad but without the provincial borders. For me, the army represents a level of energy that can result when the founding people of Canada work together towards a common goal, and this was never more clearly demonstrated than on July 20, 1992.

The Sarajevo airport had been open for humanitarian flights, off and on, since the first of July. We were bringing in approximately two hundred tons of food every day and it was being distributed in and around Sarajevo to the predominantly Muslim population.

Security for the airport was primarily provided by the First Battalion of the Royal 22nd Regiment, the "Van Doos," commanded by Lieutenant Colonel Michel Jones. They had arrived in Sarajevo from Croatia on the second of July. Michel commanded a large battalion by Canadian standards with over eight hundred personnel. He had two very large rifle companies numbering well over 250 soldiers each. Due to shortages in personnel when his battalion was being organized for deployment to Yugoslavia from its Canadian NATO base in Germany, one of the rifle companies was manned entirely with members of the Royal Canadian Regiment (RCR). And so we had a mini-Canada with the linguistic percentages reversed—the francophone Van Doos at 66 percent and the anglophone RCR at 34 percent.

After approximately two weeks of food delivery to the population of Sarajevo, I was concerned about our ability to retain the perception of impartiality as dictated by our Security Council mandate. We held and operated the airport only because the Bosnian Serbs permitted us to do so, yet all the incoming humanitarian aid was going to their enemy, the Bosnian Muslims, the primary victims in the area.

There were areas in and around Sarajevo where Bosnian Serbs were isolated and food supplies were short. In an attempt to reinforce our impartiality, I ordered Michel to make plans for a food delivery to a Bosnian Serb enclave on the south side of the city. He, in turn, tasked the RCR company commanded by Major Peter Devlin to carry out the mission.

A reconnaissance party of four Canadian armoured personnel carriers and three jeeps were dispatched on the morning of the twentieth of July to check out the route into the one Serb-held area and to make contact with the Bosnian Serb humanitarian agency that would be responsible for the distribution of the aid. Just as they crossed the Miljacka River, which cuts Sarajevo from west to east, they were blocked by the Bosnian government forces, surrounded and held at gunpoint. Anti-tank weapons were aimed point-blank at each of the Canadian vehicles. The RCR soldiers cocked and aimed their weapons and prepared to defend themselves. A good old Mexican stand-off ensued over the next hour while Major John Collins from Michel's battalion headquarters attempted to negotiate a settlement at the Bosnian Presidency with the minister of defence.

I first heard about the incident about an hour after the soldiers had been stopped by the Bosnians. I went immediately to the Presidency and was shocked when the defence minister accused me of trying to smuggle "Yugoslavian arms and ammunition" to the Bosnian Serbs. I flatly rejected his bizarre charge and invited him to join me for a visit to the scene of the stand-off where we could personally inspect the vehicles together.

The minister was no fool and knew that the incident was taking place very close to the lines of confrontation. He, quite rightly, assumed it would be dangerous for him to venture so close to the Bosnian Serb snipers—so he sent his deputy!

Major Collins accompanied the minister's delegation to the site while the minister and I remained in his office executing our own version of a stand-off. (I spent most of my time silently praying that someone in Ottawa hadn't bought any ammunition from Yugoslavia for us over the past four years.)

Major Collins and the minister's representative returned after approximately thirty minutes and reported, much to my delight, that all the ammunition in the vehicles was made in Canada except for our USA-fabricated light anti-tank weapons. There was absolutely nothing that was made in Yugoslavia nor was the amount of ammunition in each of our vehicles more than that normally carried by Canadians on operational duty.

A nasty situation had been avoided but not before the lives of our twenty Canadian soldiers had been put at serious risk. After venting my anger and frustration at a chagrined minister, I figured that was that and returned to my headquarters a few kilometres away. It was there that I found the Canada we must never, never let slip away.

The parking lot behind the headquarters building was clogged with armoured vehicles and scores of soldiers fully dressed and equipped for combat—they were all Van Doos.

While we were negotiating at the Presidency, word had gone out within the Van Doos that there might have to be a rescue mission. The RCR group being held by the Bosnians was not strong enough to fight its way out and, therefore, headquarters was considering the option, an extremely dangerous option, of sending a large tactical unit to fight its way in to the RCR group to reinforce or rescue them.

On hearing that their RCR colleagues were in danger, the Van Doos were tripping over one another to be part of the rescue team. The competition to be part of the operation was so intense that tempers were still a little frayed when I returned with the news that the situation had been defused.

Now the more skeptical observer might suggest that, soldiers being soldiers, they just wanted to be involved in a serious scrap, or perhaps the Van Doos merely wanted the bragging rights that would accompany any successful rescue operation. I don't buy into such theories, primarily because it's only natural that the closer a soldier gets to a high likelihood of serious injury or death, the more selective he or she is about volunteering for anything! This would have been a very dangerous operation, and every soldier knew it before he stepped forward to volunteer.

What I observed that July afternoon in one of the world's hell holes was the synergy of Canadians reflected in one of its national treasures—the Van Doos. At that moment in time, in the shadows of a common threat, a French-Canadian infantry battalion with a large anglophone component became more than the sum of its parts. It had an energy and a single-purpose dedication that would have played havoc with any adversary. Although outnumbered at least a hundred to one, it probably would have pulled off the rescue. I doubt very much if an entirely francophone or anglophone battalion would have given me the same level of confidence!

Canada, like that Van Doos battalion in Sarajevo, is so much more than the sum of its parts. When I'm reminded on a daily basis that one of our largest constituent peoples is discussing leaving the whole and going its own way, I fear that unique Canadian synergy will go with it—and we will all be the lesser for the parting.

Some have suggested that Canada is the most popular destination for refugees because we are known as a "soft touch" or a wayside stop en route to the USA. Sorry, I don't buy into those theories either. During my thirty-three years of wearing Her Majesty's uniform, I lived and served in seventeen different countries, the majority of which were in deep trouble, if not at war. Citizens of those countries would talk about Canada as if it were some paradise set off by itself in an undisturbed part of the world. It wasn't described as a pot of gold parked at the end of a rainbow but rather as a place where real freedom existed—freedom to express feelings and political views, to practise any religion, and even freedom to be totally different, if that's what you wanted. (With some difficulty, I always resisted the temptation to be typically Canadian and explain that we weren't really as perfect as they thought before I started apologizing for our strengths.) A close second behind freedom on this list of our strengths by outsiders was tolerance. We might not have it totally right but perhaps you would like to compare us with *any* other country in the world to which large numbers of people wish to move. Perfection might elude us but no one is in a position to lecture us about tolerance, and that includes the United Nations, which occasionally tries.

People want to come to this country because of what we are as a nation, what we represent and what we stand for. Let's face it, it would take a lot more than the promise of a minimum wage to entice someone to leave a tropical climate and venture north to a Canadian winter. But try the promise of freedom and all of a sudden, minus 30°C doesn't seem so bad.

For years, I've debated with myself about why we are so complacent about our strengths. Perhaps we are somewhat like the spoiled rich kid who doesn't have the same motivation as the poor kid to try harder and excel. Maybe it's all too easy for us. Sort of like climbing a tall tree—with a big safety net to catch us if we fall. If the economy really gets bad, we can just flog some more raw materials; if our country is threatened, the Americans will defend us; if Quebec goes, we'll survive….

It's time we stopped feeding off our indifference. The safety net under our tree could well be stolen when our back is turned, and we could be seriously hurt unless we dedicate our energies to keeping this country intact—and not just up to the next referendum, but forever.

Someone once said, "Canada is the peaceful empire where people come to avoid the responsibility of a national destiny." I wholeheartedly reject such a notion. In this world struggling to find its way following the end of the Cold War, we, as a nation, have a role to play out of all proportion to our population and economy. We are obliged to provide an example of freedom and tolerance. We must continue to help those less fortunate than ourselves. It is our destiny.

Complacency and comfort are our enemies. Two weeks after I returned from Sarajevo, the front page of the daily newspaper didn't bother me any more. I had "adjusted." Pity.

We must not undervalue our God-given blessings as a nation to such an extent that we let them be taken from us while we sleep. What an unmitigated tragedy, if that were to be Canada's legacy to a world that currently rightfully envies our bounty. We can do better—we must.

<hr>

Major-General (ret'd) Lewis MacKenzie,
MSC, CD was First Commander of the
United Nations Forces in Sarajevo.

Consenting Partners: The James Bay Crees, Quebec Secession and Canada

---

Matthew COON COME

SOMETHING unusual is taking place in Canada.

The government of Quebec is going to hold a referendum on separation from Canada. And the James Bay Crees have declared that our consent is required if we and our traditional lands are to be part of an independent Quebec. We have also declared that we may decide to stay in Canada.

But perhaps my contribution to this book is also an indication that Canada wants to include aboriginal peoples in its business, in its affairs, in its work. Maybe the existence of the aboriginal peoples in Canada has been discovered.

Last year after I made two speeches in Washington about our concern, I was criticized by the separatists for going to the United States, for speaking outside of Quebec. I was surprised by this criticism because I was speaking in exactly the same place that Lucien Bouchard had given an address just a few weeks before.

I pointed out the double standards: Québécois leaders can speak in the United States, but we are criticized for doing so. I pointed out that if Canada was divisible, then surely Quebec was too. I pointed out that if a province—Quebec—had the right to determine its future, then certainly the Crees, a people who had lived in the territory for thousands of years, had no less a right.

I asked what explanation there could be for these double standards. I could find no explanation other than the fact that we Crees were Indians. Premier Parizeau reacted immediately. He told Quebeckers that since he represented them, if I called him a racist—which I didn't—I was calling all Quebeckers racists. The furor went on for weeks until people were given the opportunity to read what I had actually said.

I have been elected by my people to defend and assert Cree rights. In so doing, I am not attacking Quebec or the people who live in Quebec. The Cree people understand and respect the cultural and political aspirations of Quebeckers, at least with respect to lands that are legitimately theirs. But we cannot accept the denial of our status and rights. A majority of Quebeckers support the right of aboriginal peoples in Quebec to make their own choice if a majority of Quebeckers decide to separate from Canada.

We Crees have lived in the James Bay area since the last Ice Age. We have always identified ourselves as one people with our own language, laws, beliefs and system of land tenure and governance.

We Crees gave our lands a name—*Eenou Astchee*—long before there was a Canada or a United States. We hunt, fish and trap on its valleys, ridges, shores and waters. The land is still the greatest provider for our needs.

On May 2, 1670, King Charles II signed his name to a piece of paper and "gave" much of what is now Canada to the Hudson's Bay Company. He named these lands—which included our lands—after his cousin Prince Rupert. The real owners and inhabitants of these lands, the Crees, the Inuit and other indigenous peoples, were not asked or even informed about this deed.

Then two hundred years later in 1870, another English monarch annexed these lands to Canada, which had become a country three years before. Again we were not asked or even told. Then in 1898 and 1912, "Rupert's Land" was broken up and annexed again, this time to the Canadian provinces of Manitoba, Ontario and Quebec. Again, we were not asked or even told.

No one spoke to us for a further sixty years or so. Then in 1971, work began on Hydro-Québec's "project of the century," and the bulldozers and dam builders burst into James Bay. Still no one spoke to us of their plans for us and our lands.

Now, in the face of yet another plan for the Crees and our lands, I am speaking up to defend Cree rights. *There will be no annexation of ourselves or our territory to an independent Quebec without our consent.*

There is an obvious and undeniable logic here: If Quebec has the right to leave Canada, then certainly the Cree people have the right to keep our territory in Canada, if that is our choice. We cannot simply be traded from country to country, as though we are livestock in a field. This may have been the way things were done in the 1600s, and even the early 1900s. But all peoples have a right to determine their futures and to keep their nationality. These are fundamental human rights in contemporary international understanding. And I haven't even begun to address our rights in the context of the Canadian Constitution.

Consider this: Cree Territory is contiguous with the Northwest Territories, Ontario and Labrador. It was added to Quebec very late, only in 1912, and Quebec began to administer the territory only in 1963. In fact, in 1993 the government of Quebec held a celebration called "Thirty Years in the North." I spoke at the Quebec National Assembly on that occasion and remarked that even a young man such as I had been in the north longer than the government of Quebec.

And here the double standard is asserted again and again: "Quebec's territory," we are told, "is indivisible." "We will never agree," say the separatists, "to any change to Quebec's borders. All of Quebec territory is sacred." "Quebec's territorial integrity," it is stated, "is protected by the Canadian Constitution, and after independence by international law."

We ask: What about Cree rights? How can a territory

be "sacred" when a government has been on that territory for only thirty years? What about our Cree great-great-great-grandparents who are buried in *Eenou Astchee*? What about aboriginal territorial integrity, aboriginal rights on lands where we have lived since time immemorial and where we and the Inuit are still the only permanent inhabitants?

We Crees do not think of borders as sacred. We are part of the land. There is no other place in the world where everything—every hill, every stream, every fork in the river—is named, as it is in Cree. *Eenou Astchee* is the centre of Cree civilization, and it is inconceivable that we would cease to care for it.

The words "Cree civilization" may clash with conventional wisdom. Aboriginal peoples are supposed not to be civilized and are supposed not to have organized societies and governments. In this view, aboriginal peoples are thought to wander across the land like wild deer, without any sense of purpose or intent, or at least no purpose that could imply sovereignty, dominion or ownership.

When Quebec began work on its James Bay Hydro-electric Project in 1971, it did so without so much as a letter to our people. When we objected and sought relief from the courts, the government of Quebec took the position that we had no rights, that we were "squatters" on our own land.

We went to court and won a landmark ruling on our rights from the Superior Court of Quebec. But Quebec's highest court summarily overturned our plea for relief. The honourable justices of the Quebec Court of Appeal ruled that any rights we may have had to our lands had been disposed of when King Charles made his distant gift to Prince Rupert, way back in the 1600s!

Canada, for its part in the 1970s, adopted an official position of "alert neutrality." To this day, we do not understand how Canada's stance was consistent with the high standards of loyalty expected of a fiduciary.

Ironically, the Supreme Court of Canada stated in the *Sparrow* case in 1990 that the James Bay Hydro-electric Project was "initiated without regard to the rights of the Indians who lived there, even though these were expressly protected by a constitutional instrument." But this statement came too late for the Crees. We had signed the James Bay and Northern Quebec Agreement in 1975. We signed under the duress of bulldozers on our lands, under the duress of statements by the Quebec courts that we were squatters with no rights, and with a federal government that stood quietly by under a policy of alert neutrality.

Little seems to have changed in the twenty years since. The government of Quebec continues to deny our rights, and the federal government is still virtually silent.

It is in this disparity concerning our rights that our civilizations seem to clash, that aboriginal rights are always held to be inferior to all other claims. I ask myself: Is this denial of our rights based on ignorance of our culture and civilization, or is it simply the blunt assertion of superior power and numbers?

I do not know. We have the impression that the separatist leadership is avoiding a direct logical or legal reply to our arguments. Instead, it prefers to mock our assertions, to minimize our relevance and to deny our standing.

We are also accused of being puppets of Ottawa, of having made some kind of secret deal with Canada to thwart Quebeckers' rights. But wherever I go in Quebec, ordinary Quebeckers support our rights. Ordinary people seem to understand that you cannot claim certain rights for yourself and in the same breath deny those rights to others.

Not so for the separatist élite. As a senior elected Quebec official told our people when Premier Parizeau last returned from France: If Quebeckers vote yes in the referendum, and France recognizes Quebec, it just won't matter what you Crees think, say or do. As for the planned Cree referendum, Parizeau has stated that it would not be legitimate, because only governments can hold referendums.

The separatists point almost daily to a 1985 Quebec National Assembly resolution recognizing eleven Native nations in Quebec. But this is as far as it goes. Parizeau uses the word "nation" as a public relations tool, but then he says and does things that are a denial of the rights that flow from our status as a First Nation, the denial of the status of our referendum being a prime example.

Without any concern for consistency, the separatist leadership also claims that the secret and eventual goal of the Crees is separation from Canada. In every forum, Parti Québécois officials now state that any recognition of a Cree right to consent would create a dangerous precedent for aboriginal peoples in countries such as Canada, Mexico, Peru and Australia to declare independence and break up existing states!

It should be clear to everyone by now that we are not separatists. You have never heard about a Cree independence movement because there is no Cree independence movement. We most certainly have grievances against the government of Canada—indeed, our relationship is in need of profound reform—but we are not separatists.

Neither Canada nor Quebec has respected and fully implemented our treaty with them, the James Bay and Northern Quebec Agreement of 1975. Our relations are often poor and unnecessarily adversarial. We are excluded from the decision-making processes regarding our lands, our waters and our environment. Our lands and resources are irresponsibly exploited and even destroyed. We enjoy little benefit from the wealth they produce.

Canada has failed to live up to its obligations to provide adequate housing and much-needed funding for community operations and maintenance. We are doing everything in our power, legally and politically, to change this situation. But in spite of all this, we are not separatists.

In the Cree communities and on the Cree traplines, life goes on. Our hunting, fishing and trapping way of life continues despite unsustainable clear-cutting and the hundreds of dams and dikes that divert whole river systems and flood our lands and waters. We face mercury contamination, open-pit mining, networks of roads, waste dumps and all the other things that could permanently end the life we have lived for thousands of years.

This is what it feels like to be a Cree in northern Quebec. It feels like we are a distant colony, without control, without rights, misunderstood and resented for our constant grievances and supposed wealth.

Through the James Bay and Northern Quebec Agreement, the Crees and Inuit entered—for better or for worse—into a permanent relationship with Canada and Quebec, within a federal-provincial structure. All parties agreed that no changes or revisions could be made in the treaty without the consent of all the signatories. And this is not some ancient arrangement: it was the PQ government of René Lévesque that legislatively implemented this agreement in 1977!

Having said this, what does it feel like now to be an Indian in northern Quebec? I will tell you: We feel cheated because this treaty—inadequate, inequitable and unjust as it is—has not been fully implemented. We feel cheated because this treaty, which was to have protected us and ensured our rights in Canada and in Quebec, has apparently settled nothing at all.

The government of Quebec has told the international community that according to rules of succession in international law, it will simply assume responsibility for the federal obligations under the James Bay Agreement. Here at home, however, the government of Quebec declares that our treaty is only a "domestic" agreement, and as such, it would be non-binding on an independent Quebec. So where does this contradictory situation leave the Crees?

First, let me make it clear that an independent Quebec could not respect the James Bay and Northern Quebec Agreement even if it chose to do so. The Agreement assumes and functions within a federal regime. Quebec as a unitary state would be unable to duplicate this governmental regime, with all the inherent checks and balances that now exist, for example, in the Supreme Court of Canada, the federal Parliament and provincial legislature, and our fiduciary relationship with the federal Crown. The very fact of separation from Canada would fatally breach the James Bay Agreement, unless all the parties gave consent to its amendment.

Premier Parizeau and Lucien Bouchard proclaim that through the Agreement the Crees have surrendered their rights in northern Quebec. This is so important to them that the PQ policy on secession reproduces the very words of the so-called extinguishment provision.

There are three problems here. The first is that the extinguishment of aboriginal rights is a discredited concept, one that academics, commissions and others are consigning to history—along with slavery and apartheid—as a breach of fundamental human rights.

The second problem is that these leaders wish to pick and choose, to keep the treaty provisions they like, while repudiating the federalist parts of the treaty that would prevent the government of Quebec from making a unilateral declaration of independence. They want to deny that our treaty relationship is with Canada and the Province of Quebec in Canada, not with some other independent country.

Third, during negotiations, the Crees were never asked to surrender their rights as a people. These things were never discussed and are not part of the Agreement at all. They include our fundamental right to self-determination and our relationship with the federal Crown. How can Quebec now claim these rights were given up?

This leads directly to important questions regarding Canada's constitutional obligations: Where does Canada stand, and what is Canada doing? The answers are unsatisfactory.

I find it particularly disappointing that this country, founded on the principles of "peace, order and good government" and the "rule of law," has taken such a soft position on the status and rights of the aboriginal peoples in Quebec. I was amazed when the federal Minister of Justice said recently of the Quebec situation that it was really a "political matter" and that the legal and constitutional issues were just technicalities.

When aboriginal and treaty rights were entrenched in the Canadian Constitution in 1982, we were told that our rights were now part of Canada's supreme law. We were told that entrenchment in a constitution meant that our fundamental rights could never be taken away.

Twelve short years later, it would appear that in the case of Cree rights, even the Constitution of Canada has become a technicality that can be invoked or dismissed at the whim of governments. I am left with the sick feeling that governments can pretty much do what they want.

It is particularly unfortunate when our fiduciary, the government of Canada, takes this position when it is called upon to confirm our constitutional and treaty rights. It seems fair for the Crees to ask: What more important and significant event could occur that would compel the federal government to act? Is not the threat to remove the Crees and our territory from Canada sufficient cause to confirm and guarantee our rights? Is Canada prevented from action by the magnitude and finality of the threat? For if that is the case, our fiduciary is relinquishing its authority at the very moment it is under the strongest obligation to speak and act on our behalf.

Are our rights under treaty and constitution mere technicalities? I don't think so. The polls show that a significant portion of the people who would vote yes in a Quebec referendum would instead vote no if they thought that the Cree and Inuit territory in northern Quebec would remain in Canada.

Let me be quite specific about some of my concerns. Section 2.15 of our treaty provides that the consent of all of the parties shall be required for any amendment to it. Section 2.11 of our treaty affirms that the Crees and the Inuit shall continue to enjoy the rights of Canadian citizens. Many other sections of our treaty confirm the special relationship between the Crees, the Inuit and Canada. All these provisions are treaty rights in our favour. They are entrenched in section 35 of the Constitution of Canada, the highest law of the land.

At the very minimum, if they are acknowledging the status of a Quebec referendum, the federal Minister of Justice and his government should state at the same time that Quebec secession is a matter for which the consent of the aboriginal peoples will be required as well.

We are gravely concerned that there is another ugly double standard emerging with respect to our rights, this time in the federal arena.

We will continue to fight for our rights no matter what governments of Canada or Quebec do. We know that we have the legal, constitutional and moral right to choose. But for Canadians, the recognition of Cree and Inuit rights in northern Quebec has an added dimension:

By rejecting—or failing to acknowledge—aboriginal rights in northern Quebec, Canada may be throwing away both a legal obligation and an opportunity that, if acted upon, could help to keep Canada together.

It seems strange to me that at this moment when Canada is threatened by the overt expression of a separatist project in Quebec, it continues to view the full recognition of aboriginal rights in Canada as a greater threat. This doesn't seem reasonable and is hard to believe.

International legal scholars have broadly confirmed our right of self-determination, especially if Quebec separates from Canada. Even the Parti Québécois's own legal scholar, Professor Daniel Turp, has confirmed the validity of our claims, stating on more than one occasion in his academic writings that Cree rights to choose are at least equal to the rights of Quebeckers to determine their future.

The issue is not whether a new republic of Quebec will treat us well after separation. That is not the question we ask. What we want acknowledged, *beforehand*, is our right to choose to maintain and develop our status in Canada, or to choose if we wish to head down the rapids in a canoe with Quebec.

I want to be clear: We are not Canada's Indians. We are not Quebec's Indians. We are our own people— *Eeyouch*, the Crees.

When the government of Quebec makes its offer to recognize our rights in its referendum legislation subject to the "territorial integrity" of Quebec, it is denying our fundamental rights in the very same breath that it purports to proclaim recognition of our rights.

Some separatists have stated that Quebec would not be a viable state without northern Quebec. That may or may not be true. But if Quebec denies us the right to choose our nationality, fearing that we may choose to remain in Canada, it cannot claim that it has respected our human rights, or that it has respected our rights as a nation and a people. And as the separatists know better than anyone else: You cannot force a people to maintain their loyalty. The separatists would be well-advised to risk recognizing and respecting our rights. Fundamental human rights should certainly come before the so-called integrity of an entity that is just thirty or ninety years old.

In the end, the Crees will make the choice. Have no doubt about that. Even if Canada fails to guarantee our right to choose, and even if the government of Quebec denies us our right to choose, the Cree people will use their wisdom and make a decision, and the people of Canada and the world will fairly judge the outcome.

If the government of Quebec holds a referendum on separation, we intend to hold our own referendum. A Cree Commission has been mandated to hold hearings in Cree communities on the possible separation of Quebec and the implications of this to the Cree people. We want our people to have the opportunity to understand what is happening and to express their views. The Inuit have already resolved to hold a national Inuit referendum.

Let me state, however, that we do not oppose Quebec's referendum. What we dispute is Quebec's right to hold a referendum on the future of *Eenou Astchee*, the Cree Territory, and *Eeyouch*, the Cree people.

The government of Quebec firmly rejects the right of Canadians outside of Quebec to play any role in determining the future of the territory it claims. The Cree position is identical: Only the Crees will determine the future of *Eenou Astchee*.

Canada's political leaders have already declared that they will respect the outcome of a Quebec referendum. We have asked if Canada will respect the outcome of the Cree referendum. We have asked repeatedly for timely acknowledgement of our right to make our own choice.

In one response, we were told by the Canadian ambassador to the European Union that we should vote no in Quebec's referendum if we want to remain in Canada. For the rest, we have been greeted with silence. It is as though section 35 of the Canadian Constitution no longer exists, twelve short years after it was signed by the Queen.

There is that double standard poking its ugly head out again.

So let me ask: What will it take for us, for the Crees, for the aboriginal peoples to finally be "admitted" to Canada? When will we be recognized as part of this great land, able to share its wealth, its future, its government? When will the aboriginal peoples be recognized as fellow human beings?

Earlier, I wrote that I had the feeling that the aboriginal peoples had just been discovered by Canadians. I have come forward and have been forthright and public with the concerns of my people. I know that the Crees have been taken into the hearts of people in every province of Canada, and that includes Quebec.

Many who would never defend aboriginal rights have supported our arguments, perhaps out of self-interest. But many others support Cree rights and aboriginal rights because they want to preserve the rule of law and because they have a fundamental respect for human rights.

People have said to me, "What do you really want? You must want something for what you are doing. What do you really want?"

I will be concrete. The Crees want meaningful inclusion in Canada and Quebec, meaningful jurisdiction, real benefit from the resources on our lands, genuine political participation as a nation and a people in Canada. We want to have an effective say in our own back yard and to get to work to develop our region, in real partnership with Quebec, with Canada, with yourselves.

We also want to be treated like human beings. In Cree we have a word for human being—*eeniw.* I want the Cree people and all of the aboriginal peoples to be treated like human beings. But this must be understood: Our conception of our humanity is that we are a people. To treat us as humans, our status as one of the aboriginal peoples in Canada—as stated in the Canadian Constitution—must be fully recognized and accepted.

It will mean only that Canadians see aboriginal peoples as having as much right as others to govern, to share the wealth of this land, to enjoy this land, to be left in peace, to have as much say, as much respect as anyone else.

Perhaps that time has come now. Perhaps Canadians realize that our influence will continue to increase, that nothing will ever happen again in Canada without us. Perhaps Canadians realize that we are really part of this country. Perhaps Canadians realize that Canada's own character, and Canada's important decisions, can never be separated from those of the aboriginal civilizations who were here so long before anyone else.

Canada is at a crossroads. There are a number of decisions that are being made that once again involve the fundamental interests and rights of a number of aboriginal peoples, who are the only inhabitants of vast areas of Canada. The right decisions about aboriginal interests and rights can be made by Canadians acting in their own interest. But I would prefer that the right decisions about aboriginal interests and rights be made by Canadians *because they are right.*

―――⚬―――

Matthew Coon Come is in his third term as the Grand Chief elected by the Cree people of James Bay in Quebec.

O Canada

———◦———

Roch C**ARRIER**

IN the café where I write these words
It seems that everyone has forgotten how to
dream
The white blizzard of winter has driven all memories
away
We have forgotten the blazing harvests of July
In the city's traffic jams we are impatient but prefer not
to arrive
In our houses we gaze at other people's dreams
We leave it to others to live our lives
We borrow the memories of others
And if my beer could think it would say of me
This man is a bad poet
And my country seems remote to me
As if it were melting like snow in the spring

In the café where I write these words
The music provides the words that will be said tomorrow
Words that do not speak to me of us
I hear laughter laughter so strong
It pushes away time
And someone asks
Should we worry about this country's future
When the music is loud and the laughter is strong

The barman's radio rhymes off traffic news
The bridges are blocked
The boulevards clogged
My country is immobilized somewhere along the avenue
of its history

I think about my friends
Who are as strong as life itself

Whose fathers triumphed over the seas
Who have come through the abyss of ignorance
Of poverty
Who have come through despair
As my own father did
And they have conquered wild forests
They have subdued the recalcitrant land
They are strong as life strong as death
I think about my friends
They could sail across the sea but they dream of an
    aquarium
Parizeau's aquarium

I go out into the street
I no longer know if my country still exists
Beneath the night that stretches out like a blue continent
I love this city as a man loves his family
My country is the country of my family
And of my brothers and sisters who do not speak my
    language
And of my brothers and sisters whose skin is another
    colour
And of my brothers and sisters whose gods I do not know
Who do not know that I don't believe in gods
The poets must find the words that will save this country

Does this country contain too much sky
Too many seas
Too many birds too many mines
Does this country contain too much land too many roads
Too many rivers that run to the sea
Too much history
Too much ice too much wheat too much memory
Too many forests too much liberty too much peace
And are our nights too silent

Our days too peaceable
Is time too gentle when it slips over us

Are we to leave our children a shrunken legacy
Are we to bequeath to them a shrunken country

Are the Rockies the Prairies the tundra the future
Too vast to contemplate
There are some who do not want a country where
Like Terry Fox one can walk from one sea to the other
As free as the passing wind
Oh must I weep like one who wanders in a foreign land

In this immense country
Our souls have become small
I call upon the poets
The good poets and the bad
You must find the words that will save this country

I know children who are waiting like old people
For the end of their life
I know youths who are in an endless corridor
On which no doors open
I know young people who abandon this country and take
      their dreams elsewhere
I know adults who have no memory
No dreams
I know there are those who pass through this country
As if they were taking a trip to the grocery store
I know people who think that this country is not a
      country
Because it does not resemble any country
That they know

And yet we were born somewhere else

We have come here from somewhere else
We have come through seas
We have gone beyond cultures stories languages religions
We have come through our ordeals
We have surmounted poverty adversity
War
We have come to this country because it was our dream
Today
We no longer dream

And I the bad poet
I call on the good poets
You must find the words that will save this country

Our ancestors walked to the end of their dreams to attain
    this country
They walked to the end of their lives to attain their
    dreams
And their children have known a better life than their
    parents
A life without humiliation
A life in which the night promised a better day
But today I know children
Children like impotent people who have no dreams
Children who borrow their dreams from others
Electronic dreams
Children who have forgotten the dreams of their
    ancestors
Children who see that their parents no longer dream
Children who do not know that life is a dream
To be spun
Children who have no belief in the future
As we have no belief in Heaven
Children who do not believe in the future
In a country as vast as a story still to be written

And I the bad poet
I summon the hundred ninety-nine thousand poets of
    this country
I summon you
To invent for those children
A dream that will save this country
Invent a dream that will save the children of this country

I walk through my city which is not very fond of itself in
    the winter
Though in summer it dances all night long
And I tell myself this country must endure
From the ice floes of Newfoundland to Victoria's sea lions
This country must endure
From the grapevines of Niagara to the Arctic permafrost
This country must endure
From the Chinook of Calgary to Quebec's *noroît*
This country must endure
From the mines of Cornwallis Island to the lute-maker
    on Montreal's rue Saint-Denis
This country must endure
From silken lacework to the visions on a virtual screen
This country must endure
From sea to sea
This country must endure
We have come from elsewhere
And we are different
As brothers and sisters are different
And we must live together in this country
As humans have to live together
Different
On the land of the future

This country must endure
Different peoples

Peoples with diverse music
Peoples who speak every language
Peoples who can speak to all the gods
Enemy peoples
Have come to this country and made peace

This country cultivates peace
Just as it produces oil wheat electricity
For it already resembles what the future will be on this
    earth
This country must endure
So that tolerance and peace will reign between a
    continent's two shores
This country must endure
Starving, thirsty women and men will continue to come
    here
This country must endure
To provide for this planet a refuge for peace
And I the bad poet
I am calling now for help
The poets must find the words that will save this country.

---

*Roch Carrier is the author of many books,
including* The Hockey Sweater Story
and Prayers of a Very Wise Child.
He is currently director of Canada Council.

Translated by Sheila Fischman

A Trade Unionist's Perspective: Democracy and Solidarity

Bob WHITE

I WRITE as the leader of the Canadian Labour Congress, a workers' organization, many of whose affiliated unions have members both inside and outside Quebec.

This organization has, at key moments in the relationship between Quebec and the rest of Canada, taken decisions that reflect clearly the right of Quebec workers to self-determination and that reflect just as clearly the desire not to have anything break the bonds of solidarity that are so critical, not only between workers in Quebec and the rest of Canada, but also among workers around the world.

We can be proud of the manner in which the labour movement, through the CLC and the Quebec Federation of Labour, has articulated a vision of tolerance and openness with respect to the future of Canada and Quebec.

In 1978, at the Canadian Labour Congress convention, delegates adopted by a large majority the "Statement of Quebec-National Solidarity." It expressed a hope that dialogue would lead to a restructuring of the relationship between Quebec and Canada to build a new and vibrant Canada and included this statement: "We, the workers of Quebec, who are members of the Canadian Labour Congress, assert the right to determine our political and constitutional future. This is fundamental, an essential prerequisite to establish the balance for future right, and we have a full appreciation of the importance inherent in our responsibility if we choose to exercise that right. We, the workers in other parts of Canada, who are members of the Canadian Labour Congress, respect the fundamental right of Quebec workers to exercise that responsibility."

In 1980, the president of the Canadian Labour

Congress discussed the first referendum in his opening speech to the CLC convention. He said, "Two years ago we had a long, intensive debate on the issue. We said this labour movement believes in the right to self-determination; we expressed the hope that, whatever the outcome, there would be continued solidarity in our ranks. And I say to you that we can debate that one from now until doomsday without ever coming to a better conclusion than that. It is the unanimous determination of the executive council that self-determination means self-determination."

Both of those important statements came as Quebec workers were preparing for a referendum vote on the future of Quebec's relationship with Canada. Before and since then, many CLC affiliated unions with members in Quebec substantially restructured their organizations to reflect the Quebec reality.

In December 1993, I was extremely proud to speak to the Fédération des travailleurs du Québec convention and to participate in the signing of a historic protocol that reflects the formal expression of a relationship akin to sovereignty-association, which reads, in part: "The CLC and the FTQ are closely linked by their history, their structure and the content of their constitutions. Together, they agree to search for ways to reaffirm their solidarity by defining new relations based on our ongoing mutual respect. In the past, CLC-FTQ relations have grown because of the fundamental interests they defend. This evolution has taken into consideration the social and cultural realities which union activities are a part of in Quebec and in the rest of Canada. The FTQ must work in a particular context, facing a union pluralism unique in this country, within a society having linguistic characteristics, where the cultural and political aspirations are different from those of the other regions. It is in this context that through the years, the FTQ has come to play a role which differs from the other provincial federations. In fact, the FTQ has long been the incarnation of the CLC in Quebec."

That protocol received almost unanimous support from the delegates to the FTQ convention and, subsequently, from the delegates to the 1994 CLC convention. I believe that, in theory and practice, the positions adopted by the CLC and FTQ with regard to Canada-Quebec relations inside and outside of the labour movement are a model of civility—a model for others to emulate.

The solidarity between workers in Quebec and the rest of Canada has never been based just on protocol or convention documents, important as they have been. Our solidarity is based on our experiences, our struggles as workers against government decisions, against the powerful forces of international capital and against transnational corporations that know no boundaries. Our solidarity is based on common struggles where we have seen the right of free collective bargaining taken away by governments in Quebec, by governments of Canada and by governments in other provinces who have had workers jailed for fighting back.

Our solidarity comes from the struggles of workers who fought historic battles like the infamous United Aircraft strike in Longueuil, Quebec, where a large multinational corporation hired hundreds of scabs, pitted workers against workers and tried to use all of its political and legal power to break the backs of those strikers. It ultimately failed, and that strike was won because of the solidarity of their union, the FTQ and CLC and the support the strike received all across this land and beyond.

I remember.

I was there on the picket lines, in the parish basement, in the local union, in the negotiations. Our solidarity was expressed when the Gainers workers in Alberta confronted an employer who once again was determined to use his political connections, the police and scabs to break their strike. And once again, because of the solidarity of the Alberta Federation of Labour and the CLC and support from all over the land, including the FTQ and thousands of Quebec workers, that victory was won.

Our solidarity was expressed in our joint fights against high interest rates, wage controls and unemployment. As recently as May 1993, thousands of Quebec workers walked across the bridge from Hull, Quebec, to join with and become part of the 100,000-strong demonstration on Parliament Hill in Ottawa to protest unemployment.

We all know that as Quebeckers enter into this pre-referendum period once again, the solidarity of workers in Quebec and the rest of Canada will be tested. There will be many who will try to divide us.

My life in the trade union movement has provided me with the wonderful opportunity to spend considerable time in Quebec and to appreciate and learn about Quebec society and the Quebec trade union movement. In my heart, my respect for Quebec and its workers is strong. I believe that we are a richer, more vibrant country, a more vigorous trade union movement, because of the participation of Quebec. And I realize that for many members of the Canadian Labour Congress outside Quebec, their desire would be that Quebec remain part of Canada and that Quebec workers remain part of the Canadian Labour Congress. But I also recognize and accept, as do thousands of members of the CLC outside Quebec, that for many Quebeckers the strongest sense of national identity is in a sovereign Quebec. That is a reality that should not be rejected in the rest of Canada but rather should be acknowledged, appreciated and understood.

But it must go further than that.

In the forthcoming referendum, the democratic decision made by the majority of those who participate must be accepted and respected—not only by the Canadian Labour Congress but also by the various political and other institutions in Canada.

If the referendum results in a yes vote, would everything then fall neatly into place? Of course not. It would mean serious, undoubtedly tough negotiations on a multiplicity of issues, but those negotiations would have to proceed on the basis of mutual respect and recognition of the new reality.

As the referendum date approaches, we must all recognize that differences exist both inside Quebec and in the rest of Canada about what the results of that referendum should be. Some of the beliefs that create those differences are held passionately by people all across this land, and we must all show respect for those differences—respect founded on shared values, shared history, shared struggles and also the clear recognition that this is a decision for Quebeckers to make.

The Canada-Quebec debate and decision take place in a global context, where national sovereignty is being redefined, resulting in the break-up of countries in some cases, and in the move towards supra-nationality in others, such as the European community.

During this debate and decision, we in the labour movement must insist that our political leadership act responsibly and with a vision that will enhance the success of our civil society in both the short and long term.

In 1976, again in 1980, and yet again during the Charlottetown debate, certain business leaders, banks and others attempted to influence the outcome with wild unfounded allegations about the economic consequences of Quebeckers' decision. It's true that a decision for sovereignty has certain economic implications, but economic blackmail and doomsday scenarios must be seen for what they are—blatant attempts to interfere with and influence the course of democratic decision making. They have no place in the forthcoming referendum. They must be rejected.

It is easy to support a policy of self-determination when sovereignty is not front and centre on the political agenda. It is more meaningful to support it when a vote on sovereignty is just around the corner.

As president of the Canadian Labour Congress and a person who believes in an autonomous, democratic, world-wide trade union movement, I know the Canadian Labour Congress will respect and accept the decision that Quebec workers take. In the future as in the past, we will stand shoulder to shoulder, women and men, in solidarity in the continuing fight for equality, equity, human rights, economic and social justice.

<hr>

*Bob White is the president of the
2.4-million-member Canadian Labour
Congress and the former founding president
of the Canadian Auto Workers union,
Canada's largest industrial union.
He is also an Officer of the Order of Canada.*

Two Solitudes Are Not Better than One!

Ivan JAYE

I GREW up in a country in which people acquired political and economic power by focusing on the differences between themselves and other groups within the society. I know what this can do to the quality of life, to the standard of living and to one's very existence. I am writing this essay to bring a different perspective to the question of Quebec separation—the perspective of one of Canada's many immigrants.

When I was very young, South Africa was about long comfortable summers, picnics on the beach, a warm sea to swim in and waves to surf on. The short, cold, windy winters were a mere interruption. I assumed black servants and whites-only park benches were the norm. The South Africa I left at twenty-one was one of apartheid, poor shanty towns, disrupted lives, disenfranchisement, tapped telephones, government propaganda and an oppressive state police force.

The England I arrived at in the sixties was nearly mythical. I lived near Hampstead Heath and worked near Buckingham Palace. The countryside was a blend of marvellous villages with familiar names such as Penzance and Tintagel, castles and churches, thatch-roofed stone cottages and gardens that had been cultivated over hundreds of years. England had history, England had the Beatles and Carnaby Street and pubs. On the surface, life was open and free. But England also had an appalling class structure that had not yet been dismantled in spite of the efforts of successive Labour governments. And England had Liz. We married in 1968. England was a feast for the eyes and the mind, if not for the stomach. It was not in our opinion a country for the future: economically depressed, too slow to change, too much past and not enough present. We left for Canada.

Montreal in that January of 1969 was harsh and beautiful. Snow in South Africa was a once-per-century occurrence, and it had snowed only once in London in the five years I lived there. Montreal was a vibrant city with interesting people and plenty of *joie de vivre*. Unfortunately, we couldn't find work. Businesses and the jobs they provided were leaving Montreal for Toronto to get away from the problems engendered by separatist activities.

Jobs were easily found in Toronto, even if a decent and affordable restaurant was not. That dull city of twenty-five years ago is very different now. Canada has also changed, for the better, we believe. In some respects we are more cautious than our southern neighbours, in others we are more adventurous. We were prepared to experiment with a more egalitarian society, and I believe we can claim a qualified success.

The advantage of coming from somewhere else is that one tends not to take for granted the prevailing conditions in one's new environment. So I look at Canada and what I see is not what my born-in-Canada friends see. I realize that a dynamic, open-minded and egalitarian society is less prevalent than we would like to think. I realize that the high standard of living we enjoy is not the norm. I know that Canada is counted by outsiders as one of the better countries in which to be living in the late twentieth century, and that four of our cities are included in the ten most desirable places to live in the world. But I also know that what this means to me differs from what it means to most of my Canadian friends. I believe that Canadians are inclined to assume—as I assumed in my early years that a white-dominated South Africa was the norm—that Canada's many strengths are a given, are built in, and are not at risk should major changes to our political and economic structure occur.

Which brings us to the subject of Quebec separation. Taking Canada for granted results in comments from outside Quebec such as "I am really getting sick of their attitude. I am tired of their constant whining. Why don't they just go and get on with it? Leave Canada, leave us to go our own way and they to go theirs." How often have you heard similar sentiments? From my perspective, the situation is far more complex than such a response would allow, and the potential losses to us all are far too great to succumb to the frustration of the failure of Charlottetown and Meech Lake. We need to take a broader view of the problem. Yes, there is a problem, and no, there is not an easy solution. But we need to be patient.

In historical terms, Quebec's problems with federalism have had very little time to be resolved, yet we are being told that a solution is urgently required. Why? We can afford to be rushed only if the cost of a bad decision is low. I believe that should Quebec separate, the loss to Quebec, to Canada and to rest of the world will be enormous.

If Quebec does separate, what will be left behind? What will be the impact on us all? Will the life of the average Quebecker really improve? In what ways? At what cost to the rest of Canada? These are the questions that all Canadians, including Quebeckers, need to ask both themselves and their political leaders. And if we do have the courage to ask them we must be prepared to challenge platitudes and doublespeak answers. The consequences of separation are too important to allow politicians to gloss over them with empty promises. Already we are falling into a trap set by some of the wilier Quebec politicians and their professional PR helpers aided by pro-separation journalists. These people insist on referring to Quebec and Canada as two entities, as if Quebec is already separate. Is there really a Canadian debt separate from a Quebec debt? I don't think so. They refer to

Quebeckers as wanting one solution to the present federalism and Canadians as wanting another. But Quebeckers are also Canadians, and the majority opinion in Quebec still seems to favour a less extreme solution. It is by amplifying differences and glossing over similarities that a very complex situation can be reduced to the outcome of a referendum held in only 25 percent of the country.

We need statesmen of the calibre of Nelson Mandela to lead us through the next few years, people who will put their personal aspirations and animosities aside, people who can see the larger picture and the value of Canada as it is presently constituted. However, in their absence we, the average Canadian citizens, must exercise our prerogative to direct our politicians to our long-term, mutual benefit. This will mean change, certainly, but change that is focused constructively, not destructively.

Canadians from Newfoundland to British Columbia have more similarities than differences. Quebec's history is just as much a part of Canadian history as is that of the other provinces and territories. Quebeckers have shared in Canada's victories and defeats, both large and small, and we are all influenced by common ideas and ideals to a greater extent than we may realize. And of course our cultural identity and economic integrity are equally under threat from our neighbour to the south.

If we allow ourselves to be smooth-talked into the them-and-us approach, we will be led by our noses to believe in a them-and-us solution. This would be a terrible error. Such an outcome will be to the satisfaction and benefit of a very small minority and to the cost and detriment of the rest of us.

We have all become too used to sound bites, headlines, thirty-second messages and instant answers. But there is not an easy answer to this issue. Quebeckers have real needs and real concerns and they must be addressed.

There is more than one possible solution, and this type of amputation is the least desirable outcome for Canada, including Quebec. Yes, it is quick and, yes, it is final, but it carries a very high price.

How does separation look against a background of current world events? Many developed countries are looking to do just the opposite—to integrate. Even France, not known for its ready acceptance of other cultures into its own, has recognized the value of teaming up with its neighbours. It has been one of the strongest supporters of a united Europe. The French saw more benefits than disadvantages in unity, yet we in Canada are in the throes of contemplating disintegration. We should be asking ourselves if we will not regret the decision to divide and destroy something that other people are struggling to create, something that perhaps we do not sufficiently appreciate.

And what after separation? Is it not likely that Quebec will want economic union with the remainder of Canada? Is it not likely that Quebec will want to be a part of NAFTA? And which is it more likely to adopt, the French franc or the Canadian dollar? Out of pragmatic necessity, Quebec may find itself as close to Canada in the new scenario as it is now, but at a significant disadvantage. It would be a small country of six million surrounded by two countries, both primarily English-speaking and with a combined population of close to three hundred million people. The alternative to some form of negotiated economic union may be considerable economic hardship and major concessions in self-determination.

If Quebec wants self-determination, what price will it have to pay for it? Will the freedom be short-lived? Will it, like France, end up believing in the value of a union with its neighbours, in which each makes concessions to the others in order that all may benefit? If that is to be the ultimate scenario, then the pain of separation should be exchanged for the pain of a continuing search for a mutually satisfactory solution. There must be a better way of redesigning what we have to the satisfaction of all who participate in it.

Nelson Mandela in South Africa is trying to build unity in an environment that is far more emotionally charged and far more complex than ours. On a different scale and in a different historical context, much of Europe is trying to do the same. Are we really so very different?

—❧—

Ivan Jaye is a business consultant living
with his family in Toronto.
He appreciates the diversity and tolerance
of Canadian society.

Kanata: Another Thousand Years

Tom HILL

Wikwemikong.
Saskatchewan.
Tyondinega.
Eskasoni.
Inuktatuk.
Winnipeg.
Mississauga.
Cowichan.
Oromocto.

A ND Ohsweken, which is my past, my present and
my future.

Canada—the land and waters, the plants and the
creatures, the Original Peoples and their Original
Instructions. And all those we welcomed, all those with
whom we share.

Do they see the Canada I see?

One summer, my family and I happened upon the
RCMP Musical Ride. In one of the elaborate manoeuvres
on horseback, the riders used a little hook in their staff
while the narrator explained over the public address system this was the way the Mounties uprooted tipi pegs to
destroy the homes of the Cree and the Assiniboine who
were blocking the construction of the railway on their
own lands.

Facts are facts, but should this insensitivity be elevated
to a demonstration of national pride? The narrator
implied the First Nations were blocking progress, develop-
ment, the advance of civilization. When I approached him
to offer my views, he showed little patience—after all, he
said, the RCMP was entitled to its historical traditions.

Do they see the Canada I see and love?

This demonstration distanced me even further from a

Canadian institution that I might have admired had it demonstrated respect for freedom and security and an appreciation of differences. The RCMP may feel more secure and comfortable surrounding itself with traditions of destroying homes, but surely it must have a better basis for its pride.

I have reflected on this incident many times, over-whelmed by the irony that we Canadians identify our-selves as beacons of tolerance, respect and human dignity, but we allow our institutions and dearly held national symbols to celebrate invasion, colonialism, domination, racism and ethnocentric concepts of superiority. *British* Columbia. Statues of Champlain. The Rivers of Thompson and Fraser. The Fathers of Confederation. "Official" Languages. An "Indian Act" still on the eve of the twenty-first century!

Why can't they see the Canada I see and love?

The Musical Ride experience took on new life in 1990 as the barricades at Oka were brought to our living-rooms and breakfast tables. One side looked across the barricades and saw terrorists, people "taking the law into their own hands," destroyers of the "Canadian way." The other side looked across the barricades and saw a century of failure to protect lands and rights, a century of double standards. Invisible barricades blocking employment, access and participation had materialized in barricades of another kind. The story hadn't changed in a hundred years—the only difference being that it was a dirt road and a bridge rather than a railway that was being blocked, and the protectors of progress and civilization rode in cars and armoured vehicles rather than on horseback.

I apologize if my words offend anyone—it is so hard to discuss the Canada I see and love with any measure of neutrality. There are too many emotions, too deep, too many experiences in an uncomfortable reality.

I should be more charitable, perhaps. I have, after all, survived. I survived, but not without wounds and scars, in the face of powerful efforts to isolate, integrate, assimilate. And not only have I survived, but the First Nations are still with us, in spite of the imposition of passes to leave the reserve, prohibition of the potlatch, the smashing of our government, the exiling of Deskaheh, the lost generation of those who were given away to strangers.

And still we love Canada, our home and native land.

We have survived the 1969 White Paper, which threatened to transform us into "Citizens Plus." We have survived multiculturalism, which threatened to reduce us to one more "ethnic group," as the British and French like to call all those who are different from themselves. We have seen parliamentary committees, ministers of Indian affairs, task forces, royal commissions, anthropological studies come and go. We are still here.

Is it possible that one day "Canadians" will become Canadians, looking to the land that sustains their lives rather than to Europe for their cultural roots? Is it possible for this young country to look back beyond 1867 and the Plains of Abraham to find its history? Is it possible that others will one day scan the shores of Lake Ontario and see, as I do, the stone canoe that brought a peacemaker to create one of North America's earliest governments, a confederacy that inspired democratic movements around the world? Why is it that Canadians know so little of the history of this land?

Is it possible for others to do what I do so often when I am in Montreal—walk to the top of Mount Royal to see how the landscape has accommodated the changes of four centuries. I imagine the palisades of Hochelaga that welcomed all visitors until European quarrels were transplanted to fester into war. Here was the original "Kanata"—the "village"—from which "Canada" derived its name. Here was the original vision—the community of shared interests—which Canada might have become, the Canada which still might be!

So many beautiful peoples in our village, our "Kanata"! Such a rich variety of faces! A treasury of culture to enrich us all with their diversity. Will there someday be room in Kanata for those who were here first?

There is still time! Our options are still open! All we need is openness on all sides, broad efforts to understand. More than any of us realize, we need a creative quest for common ground and new symbols of nationhood and identity on which our diversity can flourish.

The basis for our common ground is within our sight. It is this land we call "Kanata" that has given birth to so many truths. Kanata, which nurtures us, sustains us. It is Kanata we must embrace—the stunning landscapes, majestic rivers, immense forests, massive mountains, expansive prairies, the vast north, the fascinating muskeg, inviting valleys. That vision of Kanata has become obscured by precisely perpendicular survey lines, which so conveniently translate into artificial boundaries of exclusion.

If any of us are to have a future, we must put Kanata once again before our eyes. We must escape our self-imposed cages that separate us from one another and from our natural world, which is our common ground. We must once again become a part of the landscape, call the Earth our mother, and offer our thanks daily for her gifts to us, her children, brothers and sisters all. We are the Earth's dominion—it is not the other way around.

We must return the natural world to our mythological and spiritual thought. We must understand what it truly means when we say, "I am Canadian."

I am optimistic that others will come to love Canada as much as her Original Peoples. I have faith that we will find our solutions in our cultural expression. Over our history, our artists—particularly in the visual and literary arts—have exerted a formative influence on our understanding of our spiritual bonds with the natural world, with Kanata. It is the artists who have nurtured mutual understanding. It is art that has brought enlightenment.

It is the artists whose perceptions are best attuned to interpret the consciousness and unconsciousness of our country. It is the artists who show us what we already have, what we could have, so much better than those who sit around tables discussing constitutions and boundaries which exclude.

Yes, I have loved Kanata for thousands of years. I admit it.

How great it would be if the most significant gift First Nations have to give to our common future would be the gift of Kanata, making us once again one big village nurtured by the land that calls us her own.

Tom Hill lives on the Six Nations Grand River Territory. He is an artist, curator and writer and is currently the museum director at the Woodland Cultural Centre.

The Bear
in the Bedroom

Lesley CHOYCE

QUEBEC, I too am a separatist. All my life I have been striving to be independent, to set myself apart from large chunks of society. I equate the desire for separation with those desires for freedom and independence that are the very engines of creative human growth. And yet I find myself sitting here wanting desperately for you to stay with us. I want you to be Québécois but also Canadian because I am Canadian and I need you. My concern is selfish in nature, and I own up to that from the start.

I embrace diversity. I am a happier person in a society where people do *not* all think like me, speak my native language or live by the precise daily rules that I have been brought up by. To be surrounded entirely by white Anglo-Saxon Protestants like myself is an unhappy state. I need diversity in order to grow, to avoid stagnation. French Canada is a part of my psyche, occupying a healthy presence even though we already live apart. Acadia keeps me company and gives me comfort here in the province where I live, but Quebec is with me in my very image of myself and who I am as a Canadian.

But before I start to sound like a pompous, arrogant patriot, let me say that I am an immigrant, one who has separated from the country he was born into. Seventeen years ago I moved here for a jumble of reasons and immediately recognized this nation for what it was: a large, unwieldy, awkward country of twenty-some million people who were never quite sure of what it meant to be Canadian.

How refreshing this was after living all my life up to that point in the United States, a country rigid with certainty. My America was *certain* that it was the greatest nation on earth; it was certain that belief in the flag and the president would always lead to right action and that any American, if he or she had the gumption, could achieve whatever one desired and go on to become a billionaire or a president or both.

I grew up in New Jersey in the fifties and sixties. Nobody ever spoke of New Jersey seceding from the union. We saluted the flag each morning dutifully and pledged allegiance to the government. In history class, I was taught that there had been no separatists among us since the South had lost the Civil War.

I knew little of Canada and less of Quebec, even though it was a short ten-hour drive north of where I lived. The year I graduated from high school, I had grown curious about the north and drove with a friend to Nova Scotia, where we discovered a remarkable uncrowded coast with empty beaches and deep blue seas. The people were polite and gentle compared to where I had come from. Those who spoke English spoke in dialects unfamiliar to me, and my high school French was of little value with the Acadian descendants whom we happened upon. But I went away with the feeling that Canada had been kept a secret from me. From my brief encounter with this different place, I had decided that I had stumbled on Utopia.

I returned to America and the nation's obsession: violence. Vietnam, whose conflict I had tried to ignore for years, was no longer something I could insulate myself from. Friends from my home town were dying over there in Asia. If I was not careful, I too might be drafted into military service. I had always believed in my country— the morning devotions to the state had worked to a degree. But now everything was different.

So far, I had found avenues of deferral to avoid being drafted into the army but then the rules of the game changed. Draftees would be determined by a simple lottery of birth dates. My birthday drew number 146. If the body count grew high that year, I might find that my time was up. A formal request for conscientious objector status was turned down, and I considered the options: go fight in a war I detested, go to jail or find sanctuary in a sympathetic foreign nation.

I never was drafted, but I knew where I'd go if the letter had arrived: Canada, quite probably Quebec. I had received reports about the many draft dodgers in Montreal. I knew by now that a humble exodus was a far nobler human endeavour than taking up a gun to kill strangers or being killed for an unjustifiable cause. With a pen, I traced the green line of the New York Thruway north to Quebec and north to freedom. I had watched the newsreel footage of the American evaders and deserters in Montreal, and I had great admiration for what they had done.

Canada loomed in my mind again as something as close to Utopia as I could imagine in the twentieth century—a country free of the rabid pestilence of patriotism that seemed to be what was destroying my own sad, stubborn country from within.

Over those final years of the war, I suppose I had become a kind of separatist. So I understand that feeling well. Among the nation-wide rabble of anti-war protesters, we had set ourselves apart. We had no single unit of geography to declare independent but we wrestled Middle America into sanity of sorts until the war ended.

Even after Vietnam had ground to a halt, however, I could never fully resettle myself as an American. I could still imagine another time line where I had followed the Thruway north and gone over the line into Canada, smelled the freedom of the countryside north of the forty-ninth parallel, gone to live in Montreal or rural Quebec among a French-speaking people who would not have judged me a coward for refusing to fight in the cruel blood-bath of south-east Asia.

It wasn't until well after the war, during the winter of 1978, that my wife, Terry, and I drove to Montreal and hiked to the top of the mountain, retreated to the warmth and beauty of the botanical gardens and savoured the wonderful feeling of this "foreign" French culture on my American doorstep. When my car broke down, I confronted the language barrier head on, sampled a snub or two at my monolingual limitations, but soon found that these barriers quickly dissipated. It was a thrill to realize that Quebec was another world so close to where I'd grown up but so different.

Yet I knew virtually nothing of 1759, of Quebec's past, of deep-seated grudges, Anglo-Canadian paranoia or even of what Pierre Trudeau was calling "certain centrifugal tendencies" throughout the northern land. Instead, we found ourselves attracted to Canada as a possible alternative to life in those United States where we had grown up and grown disillusioned.

Terry and I had tested the waters several times with extended pilgrimages to the north. Shortly before we moved for good to Nova Scotia, we were camping near Point Michaud, a great wide, sandy crescent of a beach on the south coast of Cape Breton Island. In a tavern we met a young couple from rural Quebec. We sat and drank Labatt's and talked ourselves into serious mutual respect. They lived in a cabin in the Laurentians, they said, and had no electricity. These hardy Quebeckers cut and burned six cords of firewood each year to stay warm. They lived apart from urban Quebec and happily so. We became great friends but soon went our separate ways along the coast. For me, they had confirmed my suspicion that Quebec was a domain of adventurous, sturdy individualists with generous hearts and large spirits.

Our ultimate immigration to Canada in July of 1978

was that necessary act of separation from the country where I was born. It was a chance for a new life in a new country. The truth is: I immigrated to Nova Scotia, not Canada. I needed the sea, and I needed a place to live apart from the east coast megalopolis, and Nova Scotia was it. Since it was politically designated as part of Canada, I learned to become a *Canadian* as part of the bargain for the real estate.

Over the years, Canada has never tried to *Canadianize* me. I did half-heartedly swear allegiance to a queen with whom I was completely unfamiliar and felt a little foolish in doing so as I became a citizen, but no one ever expected that to be more than a symbolic gesture. Unlike America, Canada has never tried to bully me into being anything other than what I wanted to be: a writer, a surfer, a teacher, a lover and a father.

Canada is a big, shy, slightly embarrassed country. And I have loved her for this. The very ambiguity of this country (as I see it) is part of what makes it so great. And now, suddenly, I realize that it is this very ambiguity that may allow you, Quebec, to readily draw away from the rest of us and into yourself. And I feel a great sadness for this possible loss.

I would like very much to do something about it. I would like to be able to say that you have misinterpreted history, that you should forgive any sins of the past. The novelist H.R. Percy once wrote a thought-provoking short story called "Letter from America" about a francophone North America. The year is 1975 and Percy has visualized the continent as it might have been if the French had won the struggle for North America. A small militant English-speaking minority is plotting a revolt. Published first in 1976, Percy's tale provided me with some intriguing insight into the revolutionary current then stirring in Quebec. What would it feel like to be part of a language minority in this continent with the burden of a painful history on my back? Perhaps I too would have been a separatist, a revolutionary.

Perhaps, like you, I do not trust history. I do not trust it to be true. I cannot question every date, every leader, every battle, every treaty, but the more I look at the past, the more I see that the story-line, the plot, has been selected and edited. The past is a mutable thing. I have no faith in school textbooks or tomes by scholars with a conservative, Marxist, feminist or otherwise slant. I find my own heroes and villains now, and they don't coincide at all with the heroes and villains of the history books from as recently as 1970. Here in Nova Scotia, I discover that the famous early governor, Charles Lawrence, was more criminal than creditable. This renowned man, considered to be a powerful shaping influence of this province, was a perpetrator of genocide, banishing the Acadians and offering rewards for the scalps of Mi'kmaq people here. I find myself angry at those teachers and historians who have tried to skew my vision of the past, suggesting he was simply an astute military leader doing his duty. Actually, I am far more concerned with the future than I am with the past. I can't change the past but I *can* attempt to have some minor influence on things to come. I can yet remind the people of Quebec that I need them. Perhaps you feel you have no particular need of me— another Anglo immigrant, a Nova Scotian, just another *Canadian* outside of Quebec. Why don't I keep my mouth shut and let things happen as they may?

What's my problem? Why should I worry? Why do I need Quebec? As an Atlantic Canadian, it would be pragmatic and obvious of me to say that geographically we will be cut off from the rest of the country if Quebec separates. What will be left of Canada will be a diminished nation more vulnerable to economic and cultural absorption. We would very quickly become even less different from Americans than before; we will no longer have the powerful interweaving of our dual language cultures. We will no longer have the distinctive cultural intensity of Quebec art, music, writing, dance, cinema and even politics.

Should you leave us, Quebec, I fear I might end up living in the United States again without even leaving the living-room of my own house. That's part of it. Or if Canada suddenly decides to become more "Canadian," I fear it might be the Canada of a Preston Manning or a Ralph Klein. These poorer provinces of the far east might have little hope if we are dominated by Reform ideas that can reform us into economic oblivion. Why not then, at that point, simply cut the ties between east and west and become another state?

The answer is that we'd be more like a third-world colony for American exploitation than another state. And we may have some common ground with the coastal dwellers of Maine, but I believe the ties are much greater with the fishing villages of the Gaspé and Lower North Shore of Quebec. My personal geography is this salt-watery village that extends from Yarmouth to Glace Bay, on to Twillingate up to Labrador, Blanc-Sablon to Sept-Isles, Miscou Harbour to Grand Manan. This is what I see in my mind and where I live is who I am. That great St. Lawrence shore of Quebec is part of my identity and to lose you, Quebec, would diminish all Atlantic Canadians who have shared the life of the winds and tides of this coast.

I will admit to you that I have had fantasies of political independence for Atlantic Canada. I know I am not alone in this. Most Nova Scotians did not want to even join Confederation. As far as I can tell they never gave popular assent to it. Some say that the people alive in this province back then were simply tricked into a union with the rest of Canada. But that was well over 130 years ago, and I'm satisfied that the Upper Canadians and Bluenose politicians who got us into this are dead and gone so I'll let them sleep. I can find none of them alive to argue this point with.

If Quebec separates, why not Atlantic Canada as well? In some ways, this is a happy thought. The economists would say we are too small: not enough people, not enough money, not enough industry nor any combination of all the right resources. Yet two and a half million people sounds like plenty of folks. Heck, Iceland only has 230,000 or so and they've been a sovereign nation for hundreds of years. Or perhaps we could broaden our own horizon and come up with a new nation that includes all of the Atlantic provinces, Iceland, Greenland, and possibly even the Faeroe and Shetland islands could be persuaded to join as well. I would then be satisfied with cultural diversity, yet we would all be linked by our mutual relationship to the sea. The new nation of Atlantica would replace, for me, one complex unwieldy continental nation with a commonwealth of the ocean. But I doubt I could muster much support for such a nation state.

So I'm back to holding on to the highest of hopes that for me and Quebec, the future is still more important than the past. If we subdivide Canada, all of us, Anglo and French, will turn over the reins to our economy and our culture, our politics and our dreams to the corporate and political giants who can sell to us and ultimately consume us. Canada has lost much ground since I have moved here. It has become less Canadian. And already I'm nostalgic. My nostalgia for a missing Quebec will be immense.

Hiking in your Gatineau hills last summer, I was reminded of your beauty. A friend of mine who is an editor with *Canadian Geographic* drove us out of stodgy old

Ottawa and into the Quebec countryside, where we parked and hiked until we came to an imposing rock face. This was not the world's greatest challenge, but challenge enough for two desk jockeys with a few aches and pains and bit too out of shape to simply scale the wall easily. Yet we both had a hard time just walking away from it, so with caution, we climbed from crevice to cranny, ledge to ledge, several hundred feet up. First my friend would boldly go forward and then, once secure, he'd offer me a hand and I'd follow. Then we reversed the roles and I ascended and offered him a hand. Looking back from the top, we agreed we would have never done this alone. There was something in the psychology of advance and assist, reverse roles, advance and assist, that allowed for this small feat.

The view of the Ottawa Valley and the Quebec farm-land was stunning and I am thinking now of you, Quebec. I am thinking of us all climbing up the danger-ous ledges of the future. If one of us falls, it will be because the other was not there to hang on. To be quite honest, I expect your people will fare better than we Atlantic Canadians, should you choose to separate. Perhaps my request to remain with us in Confederation is merely an act of desperation; or perhaps it is the request of a climber afraid to go higher without companionship. I'm not sure.

Like your separatists, Quebec, I am very aware of what I *don't* want to belong to. I do not belong to the Liberal Party, the Progressive Conservative clan, certainly not the Reform Party, and the NDP could tempt me but I'd rather be unaligned. I do not officially belong to any denomination of religion or espouse any easily identifi-able philosophy. I am happier with my lack of affiliations than I am with organizations I am affiliated with. I am a confirmed idealist who attempts to live a life unstruc-tured, uncluttered and unencumbered. And I fail this objective more often than not.

Canada is a country that tolerates my eccentricities more than most would, I believe. I love the ocean and I love to ride my surfboard on the waves that roll up from the deep and crash near the shoreline. I surf in the summer and winter. My neighbours think I am crazy for this. Surfing at minus 20°C must certainly be evidence of madness! And yet they approve.

I grow older and happier in this atmosphere of gentle tolerance. I am surrounded by opinions on TV, in the papers and among friends and colleagues. We are all encumbered with the news of national debt and impending disaster and yet I walk upright and I go to work, I write, I surf, I tuck my kids into bed at night and I find, at the end of the day, that I have chosen the best country in the world to live in.

Each man and woman in Quebec who feels like me at the end of the day might wonder yet if it could be even better after separation. That possibility must be tempting. But I fear the sacrifices could be much greater. Some of us would still be your friend. I could not help but be otherwise. But there is always an unhealthy chunk of any population that wants to lay blame, stir up prejudice and hatred. Should you leave us, Quebec, those voices in the remnants of Canada will be much louder, more persuasive. When the next thing goes wrong for the government of the nation (and there will always be a *next thing*), someone with a loud voice and a narrow mind will want to put the blame on you. This is not really your worry, I understand, but it is mine. Canada will not have you to speak back from within, to enlighten us with the multifaceted truths, to remind us of the importance of diversity and tolerance for one another.

You may suggest to me that I have no right to say these things. I have no argument at all; I am requesting a personal favour—me, a person you have not met who knows relatively little of Quebec and argues fuzzy notions that have something to do with alternate time lines, mutual respect, geographical realignment and winter surfing.

Again I remind you that my personal republic (the one that exists inside the map of my brain) is that circle of the coastal communities along the Gulf of St. Lawrence, the Bay of Fundy and the outer Atlantic. I've travelled the perimeters of this kingdom, and nowhere have I felt more at home than on the Lower North Shore of Quebec. In April of 1990 I was fortunate enough to find myself on an author's book tour that took me from Sept-Isles to Blanc-Sablon. Michel, from the regional library system, escorted me as we travelled by plane, helicopter, skidoo and car to communities along the coast. I was privileged to meet along this shore people of French and English descent who lived their distinctive and interesting lives apart from the mainstream of society to the south. Every day of my trip was pure adventure, and I grew to respect those hardy souls who carved out happy lives along the Lower North Shore.

I identified with their love for this rugged land and the sea. I met a man in Chevery who made his own boats from the planks that he himself had cut from the trees in the nearby hills. He told me that he would never consider making a boat any other way, as if any piece of wood not cut by his own hands couldn't possibly be trusted if he wanted his craft to float.

I was met with open arms and generosity from Wolf Bay to Blanc-Sablon. I hiked to the top of a mountain at Mutton Bay and sat among the orange lichen and moss-covered rocks on a bright sunny day and felt myself to be somewhere in the suburbs of heaven. The next day, taking off in a small helicopter from a platform made from twin sheets of plywood, we flew low over the snow-covered tundra with the mail-bag hanging below. It was cramped quarters with too many passengers and a pilot who looked like he was just barely old enough to shave. When the door at my elbow flew open, everyone hung on to me as I stared down eternity and frozen muskeg and I felt truly like one of the family. Afterwards, we all laughed; then the matter was re-evaluated in two official languages, and I owned up to the fact that I felt at that moment truly alive.

I enjoyed having these northerners discuss the cities of the "south"—Toronto, Montreal and Ottawa—and wonder at how anyone could live at such close quarters to their neighbour or how it was possible to endure such intense heat in the summer. I became familiar with the bumpy ride in the green boxes of the snowmobile taxi and the taste of Arctic char and stories of the immigrants to these shores—the old Newfoundland families from the east and the French from the south-west.

It was, to my mind, a land of many blessings twice removed from the urban landscape of the continent below. Like other trips to remote areas, the farther I travelled from so-called civilization, the more *Canadian* everything felt. And it was good to be a Canadian in Quebec.

I encountered only kindred spirits and kindness in people from Chevery, Mutton Bay, Tête-à-la-Baleine, La Tabatière, Saint-Augustin and Middle Bay. I savoured the deep snow and high rock cliffs, cracked windshields and howling winds, curious kids and everywhere the lending of cultures ancient to modern.

At the final leg of the journey, Michel and his friend Kenneth settled me comfortably in the Motel Anse-Aux-Cailloux in Blanc-Sablon. After I had visited the local schools, we had a beer at the Blue Moon Disco and studied the sparkling blue white jumble of ice just outside the windows, the ice of the Strait of Belle Isle that separated this part of Quebec from Newfoundland.

For the first time on the trip, I found myself in a crowd of strangers all talking French. I was being ignored and I had no way into the conversation. Michel, comfortably bilingual, had grown animated in his talk, and there was nothing I could offer as part of this discussion. It was purely unintentional and amazing that this moment had not happened before in my life but, as I stared across the frozen strait, sipping a beer, I thought of H.R. Percy's story and I felt the isolation of language. I could understand much of what I heard but was not fluent enough to jump in, so I had now been relegated as an outsider, an invisible one at that.

That night I opted for the isolation chamber of my motel room while the snow swirled around my doorway outside. Fearing I'd be lost again in the evening's conversation, I'd stay in and sleep instead of going out on the town. But I guess Michel and Kenneth felt sorry for me and realized that I was missing out on the fun.

So, at some point in the middle of the night, they borrowed the pass key from the motel clerk and crept into my room. Silently they stationed a bear at the edge of my bed. It was a taxidermist's pride and joy, this six-foot black bear with perfectly sculpted plaster teeth and dark glass eyes, positioned in full attack posture, fierce and ready to pounce.

Then they went back to their room next door and waited to be awakened by screams.

I awoke shortly after dawn, and there within the frame of my view as I cracked open my eyes was this terrifying creature about to pounce. I don't know why I didn't scream but some deep-down primitive instinct told me this bear was not alive. It was not a threat. As I sat up, I quickly realized what had gone on here. And I knew that someone would be listening for my scream.

I puzzled for a minute what to do. Was this just a sensational practical joke? Or was it something else? Sure, it was one of those pranks you would play on an "outsider," someone not from the Shore. Here Michel and Kenneth had invaded my privacy and left me with this all-too-life-like re-creation of a bear. I could have had a heart attack. Wasn't that cause for outrage on my part?

Oddly enough, I felt privileged that they would go to so much trouble for my sake, that they trusted me enough to know that I would not call the Mounties, complain to the management or feel insulted in the slightest. It was a small rite of passage for inclusion into the world of the Lower North Shore. I had no choice but to scream and fulfil their expectations.

Sure enough, Michel and Kenneth came barging in through the door with their faces all lit up. I pretended to be half hysterical until I could see they were satisfied.

"Boy, we got you good," Michel said.

"Yeah, you did," I said. "That was really wild."

I don't know why the bear in the bedroom comes back to haunt me again and again. I smile every time I think about it, and I am reminded that not everyone would have gone to the trouble.

When I think of Quebec, I can see the Gatineau hills, the beautiful dark eyes of Quebec City children, the rich men aboard their yachts on a summer Sunday afternoon along the St. Lawrence, the blooming jungles inside the botanical gardens, and the cafés of Montreal. But most of all I see the black bear in my bedroom at Blanc-Sablon. For me it captures a spirit of good fun, slightly wicked, and a zest for life that is yours, Quebec.

For Canada, perhaps, you have always been the one to put the bear in the bedroom. Some of us may have felt threatened but many, like me, are thankful.

In my latest novel, titled *The Republic of Nothing*, Everett McQuade declares the independence of Whalebone Island on the eastern shore of Nova Scotia. He is tired of provincial, national and global politics and proclaims his republic to be free of any allegiance to any body of government. As a republic of nothing, there would be no leaders and no dogma. People would be free to do as they chose and to live without the interference of the complicated and debilitating outside world, waiting to encroach on them.

I dearly wish self-defined independence was that way in real life. I wish the perfect gentle anarchy were possible. But it isn't. Instead, we all live with uneasy alliances. My Canada is a dream of diverse peoples living together, never melting into a monotonous homogeneous mass society. It is a country where individualism is recognized, where diversity of culture and life-style is tolerated and even encouraged, where we can continue to live with one another and protect our mutual visions.

I don't expect we can make it without you, Quebec. Quebec, I too am a separatist and that's why I hope we can stick together.

—❧—

Lesley Choyce of Lawrencetown Beach,
Nova Scotia, is the author of thirty-nine books.
In 1993 he won the Canadian National
Surfing Championship.